Astral Projection and Lucid Dreaming

An Essential Guide to Astral Travel, Out-Of-Body Experiences and Controlling Your Dreams

© Copyright 2020

This document is geared towards providing exact and reliable information in regard to the topic and issue covered. The publication is sold with the idea that the publisher is not required to render accounting, officially permitted or otherwise qualified services. If advice is necessary, legal or professional, a practiced individual in the profession should be ordered.

From a Declaration of Principles which was accepted and approved equally by a Committee of the American Bar Association and a Committee of Publishers and Associations.

In no way is it legal to reproduce, duplicate, or transmit any part of this document in either electronic means or in printed format. Recording of this publication is strictly prohibited, and any storage of this document is not allowed unless with written permission from the publisher. All rights reserved.

The information provided herein is stated to be truthful and consistent, in that any liability, in terms of inattention or otherwise, by any usage or abuse of any policies, processes, or directions contained within is the solitary and utter responsibility of the recipient reader. Under no circumstances will any legal responsibility or blame be held against the publisher for any reparation, damages, or monetary loss due to the information herein, either directly or indirectly.

Respective authors own all copyrights not held by the publisher.

The information herein is offered for informational purposes solely and is universal as so. The presentation of the information is without a contract or any type of guarantee assurance.

The trademarks that are used are without any consent, and the publication of the trademark is without permission or backing by the trademark owner. All trademarks and brands within this book are for clarifying purposes only and are owned by the owners themselves, not affiliated with this document.

Contents

PART 1: ASTRAL PROJECTION 1
INTRODUCTION 2
CHAPTER ONE: ESSENTIAL ENERGY CONCEPTS 4
    ETHERIC LAYER.. 6
    EMOTIONAL LAYER 7
    MENTAL LAYER 8
    ASTRAL LAYER... 8
    ETHERIC TEMPLATE LAYER 9
    CELESTIAL LAYER 9
    KETHERIC TEMPLATE 10
CHAPTER TWO: ASTRAL PROJECTION, ASTRAL TRAVEL, OR OBE? . 12
CHAPTER THREE: ASTRAL PROJECTION AND DREAMS 18
    LUCID DREAMING 19
    IN ASTRAL PROJECTION 19
    ASTRAL TRAVEL DURING SLEEP.. 20
CHAPTER FOUR: THE BENEFITS OF ASTRAL PROJECTION ... 24
CHAPTER FIVE: 8 THINGS YOU SHOULD KNOW BEFORE ATTEMPTING AN OBE 31
CHAPTER SIX: PREPARING FOR ASTRAL PROJECTION 38

- *Positive Affirmations* 39
- *Visualization* 40
- *Hypnosis and Subliminal Suggestions* 41
- *Tips for Getting Ready* 42

CHAPTER SEVEN: 5 BASIC ASTRAL PROJECTION TECHNIQUES 45
- *Rope Technique* 46
- *OBE from Lucid Dreaming* 49
- *Displaced-Awareness Technique* 50
- *Watching yourself Sleep* 51
- *The Monroe Technique* 53
- *Muldoon's Thirst Technique* 54
- *Other Basic Astral Projection Techniques* 55

CHAPTER EIGHT: ADVANCED OBE TECHNIQUES 57
- *Target Technique* 57
- *Sound Frequency Technique* 59
- *Higher Self Connection Technique* 61
- *The Mirror Technique* 62
- *REM Technique* 63

CHAPTER NINE: WHAT TO EXPECT WHEN ASTRAL PROJECTING ... 66
- *Paralysis* 67
- *Vibrations* 67
- *Increased Heart Rate* 68
- *Buzzing* 68
- *Tingling/Numbness* 69
- *Sinking* 69
- *Floating* 70
- *Loud Noise* 70
- *3 Frequently Asked Questions about Travel in the Astral Plane* ... 71

CHAPTER TEN: PROTECTING YOURSELF IN THE ASTRAL PLANE 73
- *Increase your Vibration* 74
- *Avoid Trouble* 74

Fight and Seek Help 75
5 Things That Can Help You Increase your Vibration 76

CHAPTER ELEVEN: MEETING SPIRIT GUIDES AND OTHER ADVANCED ASTRAL TRAVEL ADVENTURES 79
Factors That Determine Who Your Spirit Guide Is 81
Level of Knowledge 82
Relationship Ties 82
Pre-Incarnation Contract 83
Accessing the Akashic Records 83
Tips for Accessing the Akashic Record 84
Sex on the Astral Plane? 87

CHAPTER TWELVE: HOW TO RETURN TO PHYSICAL BODY 89
CHAPTER THIRTEEN: AFTER-EFFECTS AND INTEGRATION 92
Out-of-Body Meditation 93
Journaling 94

CHAPTER FOURTEEN: ENERGY HEALING 96
CHAPTER FIFTEEN: INCREASING YOUR CLAIRVOYANT ABILITIES VIA ASTRAL PROJECTION 99
CONCLUSION 103
PART 2: LUCID DREAMING FOR BEGINNERS 104
INTRODUCTION 105
CHAPTER ONE: WHAT ARE DREAMS? 107
Why Do We Dream? 108
Some Facts 111
Dream Interpretation 113
Common Dreams and their Interpretation 114
How to Analyze Your Dreams 115

CHAPTER TWO: LUCID DREAMING 117
History of Lucid Dreaming 118
Benefits of Lucid Dreaming 119

CHAPTER THREE: LUCID DREAMING AND ASTRAL PROJECTION .. 122
Using Lucid Dreaming to Start Astral Projection 124

- SOME THINGS YOU NEED TO KNOW 126

CHAPTER FOUR: LUCID DREAMING AND SHAMANIC JOURNEYING 128
  - THE CONQUERORS OF CONSCIOUSNESS 128
  - THE NEGATIVE EFFECTS OF LUCID DREAMING 129
  - THE EMERGENCE OF SPIRITUALITY 130
  - HOW TO INITIATE YOURSELF 131
  - THE REVOLUTION OF LUCID DREAMING 132

CHAPTER FIVE: PREPARATION FOR LEARNING LUCID DREAMING 134

CHAPTER SIX: PREPARING FOR A LUCID DREAM EXPERIENCE 143
  - TIPS AND TECHNIQUES 145
  - TIPS TO EASE INTO A LUCID DREAM 149
  - THINGS TO DO WHEN YOU ARE AWARE 155

CHAPTER SEVEN: 5 LUCID DREAMING TECHNIQUES 156

CHAPTER EIGHT: HOW TO EXPLORE YOUR DREAMLAND 164

CHAPTER NINE: MEETING SPIRIT GUIDES IN LUCID DREAMS 172
  - WHAT IS A SPIRIT GUIDE? 172
  - TYPES OF SPIRIT GUIDES 172
  - FINDING YOUR SPIRIT GUIDE 173

CHAPTER TEN: 14 THINGS TO NEVER DO WHEN LUCID DREAMING 178

CHAPTER ELEVEN: HOW TO PROTECT YOURSELF WHILE LUCID-DREAMING 184

CHAPTER TWELVE: FIVE ADVANCED LUCID DREAMING TECHNIQUES 191

CONCLUSION 199

RESOURCES 202

Part 1: Astral Projection

A Guide on How to Travel the Astral Plane and Have an Out-Of-Body Experience

Introduction

Astral projection has been around for thousands of years, but it did not become known to the mainstream media until recently. Ever since its entry into the media, astral projection has become a hot topic. For some people, it is just a passing trend; for others, it is a buzzword, and the buzz will soon die down. However, astral projection is much more than that. Years ago, humans believed that the physical body was all there was to life and existence. But they were proven wrong as knowledge of another body—typically called the ethereal body, the spirit, or the astral body—has come to light. Astral projection or an out-of-body experience is used to describe the process of sending this ethereal body out, giving it the freedom to travel the universe without the physical body. Every individual possesses the ability to do this, but not all have learned to capitalize on it. The purpose of this book is to help people who have not mastered how to use this ability to their advantage.

Astral projection has been linked to both physical and mental benefits. As a result, many people have become interested in the practice, hoping to use it as a tool for personal development and growth. Due to the new introduction of astral projection to the media, much of the available resources on this topic offer very vague and mostly unhelpful information. A lot of the information does not really help anybody that wants to take the practice of astral projection seriously. Most of it is theoretical, and there are no practical examples. If you are currently reading this, chances are you are also interested in learning how to induce astral projections and out-of-body experiences and use them for your personal growth and development. The odds are also that you haven't found the right resources, which offer actual information and help you in your astral travel endeavors. Well, your search for the right guide has come to an end.

Astral Projection: A Guide on How to Travel the Astral Plane and Have an Out-of-Body Experience contains everything you have ever wanted in a book on astral projection. This book is different from every other text on the market as it includes up-to-date, relevant information that will make your astral projection dream a reality. From the first to the last chapter, this book further offers you something that other books don't: a theoretical and practical perspective on astral projection, astral travel, and out-of-body experiences. It doesn't matter whether you are a beginner who knows very little about astral projection or someone who already knows the basics—everybody will learn from this guide. With the latest and fact-based information on energy fields, energy centers, astral travel techniques, and astral exploration, this guide exhausts everything you ever need to know to get started with astral projection.

If you want to improve your awareness and enlightenment, and become a much more improved version of yourself, physically and mentally, keep reading. However, if you don't care much about personal, cognitive, and spiritual development, this may not be the right book for you. This guide is for people who want to better themselves. If you are ready to take an amazing journey of self-discovery and astral projection, read on!

Chapter One: Essential Energy Concepts

Every human is a spiritual being in a physical body. As a spiritual being, your physical body is surrounded by an "aura," an energy field consisting of seven different layers.

As a beginner in spirituality and energy readings, the statement above may seem a little confusing. However, it will not be as complicated once you know what it means. So, to break it down. Your body—the human body—is composed of different layers of energy, also referred to as the energy layers. These seven layers are separate and individual, yet they are interpenetrating. These energy layers surround your physical body, and together, they make up your aura. The aura is also referred to as the human energy field. Scientifically, the aura is called an "electromagnetic field." It surrounds the body and extends outwards in every direction, resulting in a large oval shape.

Every living organism has its aura—an energetic vibrating frequency of light. The auric field, or energy field, comprises varying colors and one specific color that covers the largest area at all times. The colors of your aura serve as indicators of your energy, thoughts, feelings, and awareness level. Usually, the auric colors are the same in most people but may vary from person to person in some cases. In a balanced state, your aura radiates a very bright and overpowering hue that extends several feet around your physical body. However, in a state of imbalance or unhealthiness, your auric field changes to a dull color and retracts from your physical body. Ideally, the auric colors should always radiate a bright hue as this represents vitality, positivity, and good health. Darker and cloudy colors indicate sickness, negativity, and a general imbalance of the whole body.

The colors of your aura are the indicators of your state of mind. Hence, each color means different things. Here are some of the auric colors and what they symbolize:

- Purple represents your level of awareness and openness. The purple in an aura typically appears as flashes of colors that integrate with the larger color blocks.

- Blue signifies the level of intuitive abilities, depending on the hue. A bright royal blue color may indicate strong clairvoyant abilities and balanced energy.

- Green symbolizes healing abilities. Having a bluey-green color in your aura means that you have dominant healing powers.

- Yellow indicates inquisitiveness. If you have yellow in your aura, it means you are going through what is known as a spiritual awakening.

- Orange symbolizes vitality. It is also an indicator of your emotions. A bright orange color in your aura shows that you are vibrant and in good health. Combined with flashes of red, it represents robust confidence in your abilities.

- Red means actions. Dark red is an indication of suppressed anger and other negative energies. In contrast, a brighter shade of red symbolizes self-sufficiency.

- Rainbow colors in an aura are typically found in natural healers, spiritual teachers, and lightworkers.

The aura exists to protect the physical body and shield your spirit from negative vibrating frequency, which may potentially harm you. The energy or auric field is the storage for your thoughts, beliefs, memories, and life experiences. The chakras and the aura are linked; therefore, the chakras affect the aura. They can initiate changes in the shape and colors of your aura. This is precisely why human auras vary from individual to individual. Due to differences in thought and emotional patterns, your vibrations are continually shifting. When you are experiencing a low-vibrational emotion, the aura dims its colors to reflect this. In the same breath, it brightens and expands its radiation when you are in an upbeat mood, and your vibrational frequency is at a high.

The seven energy layers of the auric field are also referred to as the "subtle bodies." They are distinct in themselves, contrary to the single vibrational field that many people think they are. These seven energy layers are connected to the seven chakras, and they correlate with the different levels of experience. Although you can see your physical body, you cannot see the other seven subtle bodies unless you have powerful clairvoyant or perceptive abilities. Even people who are well-versed in auric energy reading have difficulty understanding the energy layers. But you don't need to be able to see the auric layers before you can sense or feel them. All you need to know is to understand what they are and how to work with them. Once you know this, you will be able to tap into them to achieve things such as tuning your thoughts, tuning your emotions, or having an out-of-body experience.

Etheric Layer

The etheric layer is the first energy body and is the closest to your physical body. Often, etheric is used as a synonym to aura or subtle bodies. Etheric is a derivative of "ether"—which is regarded as a place beyond space. The etheric energy field is about two inches from the physical body. As a critical part of the entire energy field, the etheric energy is the first layer surrounding your physical body. Experts who have the special abilities to sense the second sublayer of energy describe it as having a stretchy feel. It is akin to a web—a web of energy that is exactly like the physical body. The etheric layer holds your physical body in place. It is where your main Nadis—tiny energy channels—are located.

The etheric layer is linked to the root chakra at the base of your spine. Its color varies from blue to violet to silver-gray. Of all the subtle bodies, the etheric layer is the easiest to see with your eyes. You may even be able to see yours when you rub your hands together for at least thirty seconds. Because of its connection to the physical body's health and vitality, people who are physically fit and active tend to have powerful etheric bodies.

Emotional Layer

This auric layer is the second subtle body, about three inches from your physical body. The emotional layer interpenetrates the physical and etheric bodies. It also serves as a bridge between the mental and physical body. It is connected to the sacral chakra and serves as a container for all your emotions and feelings. As the storage for your feelings and fears, the emotional field synthesizes and interprets your experience of the world. It determines how you react, interpret, and respond to internal and external situations, including other people's perceptions of you.

The emotional body is a spectrum of color that exists as a fluidly moving body. Depending on your emotional experience, the colors either appear bright, warm, and saturated, or dangerously dark, calm, and cloudy. The link between the mental and emotional fields is why people have different perceptions about the same situation. When the emotional body is out of balance, it is easy to misinterpret and react irrationally to situations. However, in equilibrium, the emotional field acts as the center of everything. In other words, it regulates your emotional state. Just think of it as the driver of your consciousness.

Mental Layer

The mental body is the third layer of the auric field. Hooked to the third chakra, it is responsible for the formulation of thought processes. From the name, you can tell that this layer connects with your mind, cognitive ability, and mental state. The mental layer is also linked to the solar plexus chakra, which is yellow. Hence, it takes the appearance of a golden-yellow cloud circling the head and shoulders of each person.

Your mental layer is about three to eight inches from your physical body. Still, it expands when you engage in intense thinking or thought processing. Like the physical and etheric body, the mental body also has a structure. Within the layer, you can see how thoughts form. The colors of the mental layer are connected with some colors from the emotional body. The colors linked to each other represent the emotions associated with each thought-form, which explains why the mental and emotional layers are connected.

When you focus on one particular thought intensely, the thought appears well formed, and anybody with a high sense of perceptiveness can see the thought. This gives an insight into the reality of how thoughts take on forms in the auric field and subsequently travel down in effect into the other energy bodies until they reach the forefront of your physical body. The mental layer is typically more robust in people who exercise their minds more regularly than the other senses. It takes a glowing appearance when you mentally focus on anything.

Astral Layer

The astral body sits above the three layers discussed so far and extends about one foot outward. This layer is connected to the fourth chakra, which means it is the bridge between your physical and spiritual self. It is central to all the other layers, i.e., it is positioned in the middle. Similar to the emotional body, the astral layer is home to a spectrum of light that is continuously moving. The hue of the colors in the astral body changes depending on your spiritual health. Your astral body is closely linked to the heart chakra and correlates with your expressions of matters of the heart. Therefore, it affects your relational bonds and connections with other people.

Etheric Template Layer

The etheric template sits fifth from your physical body, extending about two feet outwards. It is the energetic blueprint of the physical from—the matrix from which your structure and organs originate. This layer is connected to the throat chakra. Similar to the throat, the etheric template body channels everything on the physical plane into being. Before your physical body ever falls sick, you can feel it in your etheric template body. This also means you can heal diseases and illnesses in this auric plane before they even manifest in your physical body. The etheric template takes on different colors in different people. When you set yourself free from limitations and your self-awareness increases, the etheric templates radiate brightly.

Celestial Layer

The celestial layer is the sixth subtle body and is connected to the third eye chakra. Some people also call the celestial body the spiritual body. The celestial body serves as the bridge between you and your connection to all things, including your true self to the universe, the higher being, the divine, or the beyond. While it is one of the most powerful auric layers, many people are unaware of the existence of the spiritual body, and this is because they are out of tune with the spiritual energy. It is also the place where your imaginations, insights, and intuitions take shape. It has very little to do with religion and everything to do with your higher self. It is the place where awakening and enlightenment begin.

Ketheric Template

The seventh and final layer is connected to the crown chakra, extending three feet outwards. The Ketheric template signifies your connection with the universe. It is where you become one with the cosmos, the higher being, and the divine. It is the state of higher awareness—the place where your higher consciousness resides. Your spiritual body is a representation of the union between your soul, experiences, karma, and destiny. It contains everything your soul has experienced and will experience in your past and present lives.

The Ketheric layer holds the auric field and each chakra together. It is the interface between you and everything else. This layer is golden. Unlocking the Ketheric layer opens up the path to an otherworldly understanding of the universe and what you stand for within it. Successfully unlocking the Ketheric layer gives you the ability to access your Akashic records and view details of your past life and anybody else's.

Although these seven energy layers are distinct bodies, they can interconnect with one another based on your daily experiences.

Now, many people generally believe that the physical body is also part of the auric field, but it is not. The auric field surrounds your body. All seven layers of the energy field are "subtle bodies." The physical body is a product of the morphogenetic field. According to biology, this is a family of cells that form the body's concrete structure and organs, such as your brain, skin, flesh, bone, blood, and so on. Your physical body is your skeletal system, ligaments, veins, and everything that makes up what you call your "physical self." Because of its tangibility, you can tell when the physical body is hurt or not, healthy or not, full or not. It generally gives you recognizable and physical signs. The physical body is a representation of your physical experience in the world, physiology, and ability to hurt and heal. When this body is in equilibrium, you feel healthy, accommodating, and flexible. When your vitamin and mineral elements are in a state of balance, the physical body is free of toxicity, acidity, and pain. The seven layers of the energy field all exist to protect and shield the physical body.

Of all the seven auric bodies, the one that will be discussed the most in this book is the astral body. Without the astral body, astral projection, astral travel, and out-of-body experiences would be impossible. So, find out what distinguishes these three terms.

Chapter Two: Astral Projection, Astral Travel, or OBE?

Astral projection may be a relatively new concept in modern media, but it has been around for years. Once, it was a knowledge that only a few enlightened people possessed. Now, astral projection is in the mainstream media, and much of the information surrounding the concept is being muddled. Astral projection, astral travel, and out-of-body experiences (OBE) are being used interchangeably. This leads to misinformation for people who think they would like to travel the astral plane. The astral body and other subtle bodies have long been recorded in historical records and reports. On that basis, many esoteric healing practices have been developed in alignment with knowledge of the human energy field, especially in the East. To this day, esoteric healing practices remain widely acknowledged and embraced. They are becoming more popular in mainstream media too.

To understand what astral projection or astral travel entails, you must first have an idea of what OBE entails. An out-of-body experience is a state where you can sense your consciousness slip out of your body. In science, it is also referred to as a dissociative episode because your consciousness is dissociating from your physical body. OBEs are believed to be experienced by people who have been in near-death situations. Typically, you can feel your sense of self in your physical body. This allows you to perceive the world and everything it contains from a vantage point of view. But during OBEs, you feel like you are looking at the world and yourself from a different perspective. Unless you have directly experienced an OBE, it is difficult to give an accurate and detailed description of what it feels like. However, an OBE generally involves a sensation of floating outside your body. Also, you feel like you are looking down at the world and your body from a height. During an OBE, everything feels very real—as if you have the experience in reality. OBEs generally happen unintentionally and without warning. Plus, they do not last that long.

Many people refer to astral projection and OBE as the same thing; however, they are different. Astral projection is an intentional OBE. It involves everything that happens in a usual out-of-body experience. Still, the critical difference is that you have to make a deliberate effort to send yourself out of your body. Plus, an astral projection involves making an effort to send your consciousness toward the spiritual plane.

On the other hand, OBEs are unplanned, and they happen when you least expect them. Astral travel is almost the same as astral projection and OBE, but it is a more profound experience. When you astral travel, you succeed in sending your consciousness to the spiritual dimension. You get to stay in the dimension and tune in with your higher consciousness for a specific amount of time before you finally leave your body. You can say that OBE is the scientific term, while astral projection or astral travel is spiritual. But they all refer to the same practice or experience, with only slight differences.

There are other differences between astral projections, astral travel, and OBEs. In the scientific field, experts recognize that OBEs do indeed happen. There are several studies dedicated to the understanding of OBEs. Unintentional OBEs are said to happen for several possible reasons.

One of the possible triggers of OBEs, according to medical experts, is trauma or stress. A dangerous, threatening, or frightening situation may trigger a fear response, which then prompts you to dissociate from the situation and experience it as if you were an onlooker. In essence, when you dissociate yourself from a traumatic experience, you can watch the event play out from somewhere outside the physical plane. A lot of women experience OBEs during childbirth because of the difficulty. Another possible cause of unintentional OBEs is medical conditions. Others include medication, shock, meditative trance, and so on. However, none of these exact causes apply to astral projection or astral travel. Astral projections are intentional. They do not happen due to stress, trauma, or any of the reasons mentioned earlier. During an astral projection or travel, you can maintain a clear consciousness of self. Your senses become heightened and more refined, giving you the chance to question your actions and decisions outside of your body. Astral travels are not unexpected, and they don't take you by surprise.

With the help of astral projection, you can unlock the knowledge and power required to discover the answer to the ever-present question about life in the physical plane. Once you realize that there are other human dimensions—places of existence where you transit to after death—life begins to take on a deeper meaning. By learning how to travel the astral plane, you can learn things you didn't know about your true self and unlearn the things that you previously considered the truth. This opens your eyes to the fact that your physical body is nothing but a part of your whole self. You realize that there is more to your existence than the ordinary eye can see. Traveling the astral plane is the key to unlocking a higher awareness of yourself. In limited awareness, you do not truly see and understand what makes up your existence. You believe that the physical body is all there is to reality. Astral travel can help correct this erroneous belief.

As a human, you are born with a physical body that allows you to exist on the physical plane. Without the physical form, it would be impossible for your soul to exist on Earth by itself. Astral projection allows you to detach from this physical body and project into the neighboring plane of existence—the astral plane. When you do this, your soul leaves your physical body and enters the astral body. The astral body is already a part of you, just like your physical body. The difference is that you cannot intentionally take possession of it unless you learn to tap into the auric field.

The astral body has distinctive qualities that set it apart from your physical form. The physical body is restricted by gravity, but the astral body is not. Through mental effort, your astral body can easily overcome the restriction of gravity. While you are in your astral body, you can walk around just as you do in the physical, soar above ground, or even travel into space. Unlike the physical body, the astral body doesn't get hurt or injured. On Earth, one of the strongest fears that humans experience is the fear of pain and injury. Out of the body, though, you can unlearn the normal human response to seemingly negative emotions such as fear or the experiences that trigger these emotions. This is because nothing can damage or harm your astral body. You can't be hurt by guns, knives, diseases, or racing cars; thus, you don't respond to them in fear.

Astral projection is a form of telepathy. You could say that it is telepathy in its simplest form. When you are out of your body, you can communicate with thoughts. Verbal communication is not compulsory. You don't need to move your lips to get people to hear what you have to say. However, you can communicate verbally if you wish. Sometimes, in the physical plane, you may hear something that seems like a thought but, in fact, is someone else communicating to you from the astral plane.

There are four ways in which your consciousness can leave your physical body to enter the astral body.

- **Unintentionally/unconsciously**: You can astral travel while you are asleep, without meaning to. You won't even know that you are out of your physical body. Many people experience this form of astral projection, but they don't know it. As a result, they may not believe that astral projection is a real experience. When you have dreams of flying, it is usually because your astral body is floating and looking down at the physical one.

- **Unintentionally/consciously**: This happens when your consciousness leaves your body, and you awaken in the astral form. Without previous knowledge of the astral plane or astral projection, you may react in panic, believing yourself to be dead. This is what happens with many people who have been in near-death situations and experienced an OBE.

If this happens for the first time, your immediate reaction will be to struggle back to your body. But as you will find, the more you try, the harder it is for you to reach your physical body. The key is not to fret or panic. Stay calm, and you will get back to your body.

The reason you will find it challenging to get back to your physical body when you struggle is:

Struggling keeps the vibrational frequency of the astral body out of sync with the physical. Therefore, your consciousness cannot easily transit from one to the other.

- **Intentionally/unconsciously**: You try to project yourself out of your physical form and succeed. However, you have no idea what you have accomplished. Therefore, you do nothing until you return to your physical form unconsciously.

- **Intentionally/consciously**: This is practiced astral projection, which you have to learn how to achieve. It is when you deliberately leave your physical body for your astral body. In your astral form, you can do all the things your physical body does.

Today, many people have become familiar with and accept that they live within a universe made up of energy and matter. More so, they have become comfortable with the knowledge that they are beings of energy. Essentially, the significant difference between unconscious and practiced astral travel is that conscious astral projections allow you to control your astral body and where it visits in this state. But you have no control over what happens when you astral travel in your sleep. When you dream, it is a form of astral projection, an unconscious one, so much so that your soul leaves your body when you sleep.

There is a physical switch that can be activated at will to trigger a state of astral travel. You activate this switch when you engage in intentional and conscious astral travel or an out-of-body experience. It is located deep in the brain and is referred to as your pineal gland. When the pineal gland is activated, it releases dimethyltryptamine (DMT). This DMT is the chemical that alerts and propels your soul out of your body. It also triggers near-death experiences and initiates the passage of the soul during the time of death.

Realistically, only a handful of people can control what their soul does when it is out of the body while they are asleep. Astral projection gives you control, which is why it is called "conscious sleep."

There are numerous benefits of learning and practicing astral projection in a state of awareness. These benefits go beyond the physical or mental realm. To help you assimilate how astral travel can impact your life, there is a chapter dedicated to the benefits of astral projection, astral travel, and out-of-body experiences.

Chapter Three: Astral Projection and Dreams

People travel in their dreams, sometimes lucidly and sometimes without realizing it. As a result, many people believe that astral projection and lucid dreaming are the same. Many people claim that you visit the astral plane every time you sleep and dream. But are they? No, they are not.

Astral projection is not a construct of the mind, unlike dreams. Dreams are mental constructs your subconscious mind creates when you are asleep. You can only dream when you sleep, but you do not have to sleep to practice astral projection. When you go to sleep, you are living this reality to go into your subconscious mind. However, during astral projection, you leave this reality for another realm of existence that is just as real—a field where your physical body cannot go, but your soul can visit at will. In a dream, you come across characters that are neither real nor conscious; your subconscious mind creates these characters. They are usually people you know and are familiar with. In astral projection or travel, you come across actual beings, conscious and real. The beings you meet on the astral plane are either people who live there or those visiting, like you. The odds of meeting people you already know are low.

Lucid Dreaming

Lucid dreaming, in the simplest terms, is dreaming while in a state of awareness. When you dream, and you are conscious that you are dreaming, that is lucid dreaming. When you are lucid (conscious/aware) in your dream, you can control the characters in your dream, but this typically requires some practice. In a lucid dreaming state, you can hang out with your favorite celebrity, go hiking, and maybe even shapeshift into your pet. It all determines how far you are willing to let your imagination run. On the contrary, you can't control the beings you meet in the astral realm. Like you, they are their own beings and have free will.

Due to the similarities, lucid dreaming is often confused with astral projection. However, some differences separate them. To see how distinct the two experiences are, here is a brief comparison.

In lucid dreaming:

- You are asleep
- You are aware that the experience is a dream
- Your location can be wherever you want
- Your consciousness doesn't leave your body
- You can control the characters and environment in the experience
- When you finish dreaming, you simply have to wake up

In Astral Projection

- You awaken and project yourself
- The experience is real
- Your experience begins wherever your physical body is

- Your consciousness leaves your body, and the physical body becomes void

- You cannot control the actions of the spirits you meet on the astral plane, but you may be able to manipulate the environment a little

- Your consciousness returns to your body only after your experience is over

One thing that is highly misunderstood is that lucid dreaming and astral projection are two individual practices. You do not have to learn lucid dreaming before you can practice astral projection. Once you learn and perfect your astral projection skills, you can easily lay down on your couch and project your consciousness out of your physical body to visit the astral plane. It is challenging to learn, but it is not impossible. Transmitting your consciousness from your physical form can be learned to the point where you could leave while seeing a movie at the theater or dining with friends at your favorite spot. However, it isn't farfetched to say that perfecting your lucid dreaming skills can help you master astral projection to that point.

Astral Travel During Sleep

When you sleep, the soul takes charge of your body, with the ability to do whatever it wants and go into other dimensions. Some people experience this as a nightly occurrence without realizing it. If this happens to you, you wake up the next day with zero knowledge of your soul's wandering and travels. Instances like this are *unconscious astral travel.* Usually, when you arise from a dream where your soul has astral traveled to other dimensions, you may have a hazy memory of the experience. You may even think it was just a "weird" dream, as dreams can be weird. Other times, you probably will not even remember a thing about your soul wandering about all night. And there are times when you wake up with a vivid memory of a dream that involved hanging out with others and living life. In cases like that, you are probably wondering if that counts as a dream or astral travel. You may also be wondering how to start recognizing when your soul has astral traveled while you were asleep. As long as your consciousness leaves your physical body, it is astral travel. Being aware of your dreaming state does not count as astral projection if your soul doesn't leave your physical body.

How do you recognize when you have astral traveled in your dream?

Firstly, you may recall the dream vividly and feel like it was real. If you remember meeting people that you don't know in real life and talking to them, your soul likely traveled to the astral realm while you were asleep. Also, you may recall going to unfamiliar places. Another indicator of astral projection in dreams is when you wake up feeling exhausted like you had spent the night running errands. Sometimes, the body feels hugely unrested once the wandering soul returns to it after a night of adventures. It doesn't matter whether you had a good night's sleep or not; you simply feel unusually tired. If you remember having a dream where people didn't look like actual people, it may be an indicator that you astral traveled. Sometimes, people appear distorted and shapeless in their unconscious travels. They may appear surrounded by a blinding light and varying colors without assuming a human form.

Unless you have learned the techniques and started practicing, you can't consciously astral travel in your sleep. If you dream about astral projection, it is still a dream; it doesn't mean you are actually living the experience. But once you have learned to become conscious and astral travel in your dream, you will know when your soul leaves your body. You will know because you will be alerted from sleep. You will find that your physical body can't move, and you will feel the soul slip out of your body. You may even feel a powerful tingling sensation and hear some sound. Experiences vary from person to person, but the result is always the same. Once you are in your astral form, you can travel the material plane or move beyond it to the astral realm itself. In astral projection, you can have actual experiences with your consciousness and remember them vividly because they are real.

How to tell the difference between dream travel and astral travel.

Undoubtedly, you can travel to different places in your dreams without going out of your body. Say that you have been to Hollywood before on vacation. You went to Hollywood, visited all the famous spots, and even got to get the autographs of a few of your favorite actors. In your dream, you may get on an airplane and go to Hollywood once again. This is because you have been to this place before, and it is easy for your subconscious mind to reconstruct it from your memory box. Even if you have never been there before, your mind may recreate the memory from the movies you watch and the books you have read. In cases like this, you are not astral traveling. Instead, your mind revisits a familiar place you have seen or been before in your waking state.

- In dream travel, the experiences don't feel as vivid. Instead, they feel mundane and vague.

- You only go to places you have been before or places you have memories of, tangible or intangible, such as your high school, usual holiday spots, or college.

- You see people from your past or present—people whom you know. For example, you may see your young neighbor from ten years ago precisely as they were when you knew them.

- The dreams take on a symbolic meaning that you can analyze and interpret once you wake.

- You engage in the most random and mundane tasks in dream travels, such as doing the dishes or reading a booking.

- You transport to the location your dream travel via a standard means of transportation, such as your car or the public train.

- You verbally communicate with the characters in your dream just as you do in the physically aware world.

Can dreams be signals from the astral plane?

Some spirituality experts believe that dreams are sometimes messages from the astral plane. When you are asleep, it is a chance for the conscious beings on the astral plane to caution you about specific actions or decisions by sending coded messages via your dreams. Like most humans, you probably forget your dreams, but it helps to take notes when you awake and remember any codes or symbols in your dream. Then, you try to analyze these symbols. Usually, dreams get overcolored by the subconscious mind and its fancy illusions, and it is vital to dissect the true meaning of your dreams. An astral plane is where you can get insights and catch glimpses of things that are yet to manifest in the physical realm. Therefore, astral projection can help you gain new perspectives on your actions and the decisions you make.

How to travel the astral plane with lucid dreaming skills.

Mastering lucid dreaming comes with a positive side effect. It teaches you to wake your mind while your body remains asleep. To astral project consciously, this is a needed skill. To separate your soul from your physical body, you have to learn how to transit your consciousness from your body to its astral vehicle. It is akin to putting your soul in a ghostly body, but it's not as simple. So, once you master how to keep your body asleep while your mind remains awake and aware, you are halfway to learning conscious astral projection. Thus, it is highly advised that you first learn to practice lucid dreaming before you begin astral projection practices.

Chapter Four: The Benefits of Astral Projection

Whether you want to call it astral projection, astral travel, or an out-of-body experience, leaving the physical terrain to survey the world from an otherworldly point of view can have a whole lot of benefits for your physical, mental, and spiritual wellbeing. Many people who experience OBEs have reported the experience as being both exciting and enlightening. The reported benefits of astral travels and OBEs go well beyond the restrictions of your physical senses and intellect. After an out-of-body experience, you go through an awakening of your inner self—the one connected with your spiritual identity. You become conscious that you are more than just matter and have more awareness of reality as it is occurring. Many people have reported gaining more in-depth and profound wisdom in their personal dealings and experiences, and a sense of connection with their spiritual core. This is what OBE practice can do for you:

1. Greater Awareness of Reality

Astral projection expands your awareness of reality. If you have never left the material plane, it is easy to believe that it is all there is to the universe. Furthermore, this is what many people who have never had an out-of-body experience believe. However, your perception of reality significantly improves after you have experienced it once. This is because you meet other beings in the astral plane, some of whom have a deeper understanding of life and the universe than you. As long as you don't impose on them, the beings you meet are ever-ready to share their knowledge with you.

2. Verification of Immortality

Out-of-body experiences are the verifications of your immortality. Of course, you already know that people die. But you don't know what this feels like. Death is something millions of people experience yearly. It involves the soul leaving the body forever, never to return. OBEs provide the same experience as death because your consciousness slips out of your body completely. The difference is that your soul can return to your body after you are done on the astral plane. Conscious astral projecting is the key to gaining firsthand experience of the soul's ability to exist separately from the physical body.

3. Loss of the Fear of Death

Admittedly or not, most people are afraid of death. However, the fear of death does not seem as precarious as it usually is when you start traveling the astral plane. This is usually a life-changing realization for people who experience OBE for the first time. The fear of death stems from the fear of the unknown. *Where do we go when we die? What happens to our soul?* These are questions that you find the answers to when you have an out-of-body experience. When you visit the astral plane, you are in a psychosomatic state, which means you exist outside of your physical self. The astral self, unlike your physical self, is not held captive by limitations and fears. Practicing astral projection or merely having an out-of-body experience teaches you that there is little to fear about death as there are other existences beyond this physical one. The more you practice OBEs and astral projection, the more your fear of death decreases.

4. Increased Respect for Mortality

People who have never had an out-of-body experience tend to think that discovering the reality about death would negatively impact them, but quite the opposite happens. Rather than deaden your appreciation for the world and life as you know it, astral projection increases the admiration and appreciation for everything around you. The astral plane and the physical plane are two existences that are interpenetrating. Yet, they are both different in distinctive ways. The physical realm has certain things that make it special and unique. Astral projection teaches you to take life as an adventure once you realize that you will not have your physical form forever.

5. Accelerated Self-Development

The firsthand experience and recognition that you are more than just a physical being opens up layers of your consciousness that otherwise remain locked. This introduces you to newer levels of personal development. If there is anything that can quicken your personal development, it is astral projection. With greater awareness of reality and a widened vision of the seven planes, you start to see the world from a new perspective. More importantly, you start applying the new perspective to your thoughts, actions, decisions, and life experiences. The opening and awakening of your mind overflows into your physical reality and readies you for more of life's many adventures. Once you unlock the vast knowledge seated deeply in your subconscious mind, your ability to explore the universe at every level increases.

6. Improved Psychic Abilities

Out-of-body experiences greatly enhance telepathic, precognitive, prophetic, and psychic abilities. Every individual possesses these abilities to some extent. But they are much improved upon when you have an awakened connection to your higher self. Increased psychic capabilities come with being in tune with your energy field.

As you unlock your auric field and align yourself with its energy layers, your psychic abilities develop. Some people have reported being able to engage in *remote viewing* after they start practicing astral projection. Others have reported meeting deceased loved ones in the astral plane. Whatever your psychic abilities are, be sure that they will be heightened once you start practicing astral projection.

7. An Increased Need for Answers

After an out-of-body experience, many people develop a desire to navigate the spiritual world on a personal quest to solve certain things they have always considered mysteries. They realize that secrets only remain mysteries when they don't seek the answers to the questions they pose. Solutions are readily available for those who are willing to seek them out.

8. Accelerated Evolution

Over the years, humans have been evolving. However, this evolution is not the result of biological changes; it is the evolution of consciousness. As the physical world becomes continuously complex, humans develop an innate need to uncover the reason for the rapid changes happening around us. Hence, people's need for answers takes them into every progressive level of human evolution. Eventually, they will evolve to the point where they are finally ready to accept non-physical realms and dimensions, and explore them.

9. Ability to Heal the Body and Soul

Sleeping is a way for your body to recharge, restore, and heal. Lack of sleep can have many destructive effects on your mental and physical health. In fact, missing out on sleep for too long can result in death due to how the body cannot recharge or restore its healing abilities. Since you leave your physical form behind when in an astral state, it is similar to sleeping. As a result, practicing astral projection provides an excellent opportunity for your body to heal faster and better. Plus, the fact that your energy field is in a heightened state of alertness during astral projections allows healing to take just a few minutes in the astral state. In your sleep, healing can last several hours. More so, some OBE practitioners have reported being able to heal themselves and other people in their astral state. It often involves focusing your thought on any particular part of your body where you need healing.

10. Increased Energy Balance

When you meditate, your state of awareness dramatically increases, resulting in higher mindfulness. In the same way, OBE practice strengthens the connection you have with your auric field. It is just like how you use exercise to improve the strength of your physical body. Regular practice of astral projection puts your energy system in a state of balance, which means all your energy layers are synchronized. The more you practice, the better your energy equilibrium. Soon, training will take you to the point where your energy systems are wholly calibrated within your auric field.

11. Insights into the Past

The theory that the universe is parallel, so people's lives parallel one another, is quite popular. In short, life is not a linear reality or existence. Many people who have had an OBE often report being able to visit their past experiences and recall memories from this life because there is a residual energy point where all lives are intersected. When you visit the astral plane, you may come into contact with this energy point and watch events in your past lives play right through your eyes—talk about watching a movie where you are the main character. The only thing is that you are the only one who can watch.

12. Increased Spirituality

Astral projection deepens your connection with the spiritual. Once you realize that other things exist beyond the material plane, it is difficult to veer away from the bonding between you and your spiritual essence. OBEs provide deeper insights into spirituality and the nature of spirits. OBE is a spiritual experience because it involves your soul/spirit. You gain a sense of connection with something that appears to be far higher than you. Some people call this the universe, while others call it the higher being within everyone. Whatever you choose to call it, just know that you will awaken a more reliable and robust connection to real and significant existence.

13. Encounters with your Spirit Guides

There are non-physical beings that reside in the astral plane. Astral projection is a way of meeting these entities and beings, including angels and spirits. They may provide answers to your innate desire and solve the mysteries you are concerned about. Otherwise, their role in the astral plane may simply be to serve as your guide, directing you down the right path. Regardless, any entity you meet in the astral plane cannot hurt or harm you as long as you are in control of your astral form and energy field. So, don't fret too much about staying safe in the astral realm.

14. A More Profound Sense of Knowing

There is nothing more powerful than personal knowledge. Knowing something is much more potent than believing. Compared to beliefs, personal knowledge can profoundly inspire changes in your life. It is one thing to believe that spirit guides exist, and it is another thing to know that they exist. There is a sense of calm and confidence that comes with knowing something instead of believing it. OBEs give you verifiable knowledge about spirituality and immortality. As a result, the profound sense of knowing that awakens is better experienced than explained.

15. Personal Answers

This is one reason why many people want to learn how to have an OBE. You, like these people, want your questions about existence answered. Every human has questions regarding their existence—*What are we? What is our purpose for existing? What meaning does life hold? Will life continue to exist as it is?* These are all questions that can only be answered through a personal out-of-body experience. OBE is a powerful way of obtaining answers to all the questions you have about life and existence. There is no reason why you should settle for beliefs when you can get answers to the questions you have.

16. Psychological Freedom

If you have been struggling to break away from certain mental habits and ruts, out-of-body experiences can help you achieve this. Just the shock of being independent of your physical body while retaining control and consciousness is enough to provide you with a more enlightened view of your present existence. The expansion of your view of existence can be instrumental in awakening deeper levels of understanding and personal development.

There are many more benefits of astral projection. Still, these are to be experienced directly when you explore the world independently outside your physical form. Oh, and if there is any benefit of astral projection that most people prefer, it is the fact that you can astral project yourself to the moon if you so wish. Amazing, right? Well, you will learn all about how to do that as you progress in the book.

Chapter Five: 8 Things You Should Know Before Attempting an OBE

In case you thought that astral projection is something you could toy around with just for the fun of it, think again. Many people associate certain fears with the concept of traveling to and exploring the astral plane, a relatively unknown place. If you also have these fears, understand that your fears are valid. This is why you must know what to expect when you visit the astral realm. This chapter aims to help you understand the potential danger you may face in the astral realm. Even though people like to connote fear as a negative emotion, it exists for a reason—to protect them. Therefore, there is nothing wrong with having specific fears as a beginner who is traveling to the astral plane for the first time.

First of all, you should understand that there are people who have perfected the art of astral projection and astral travel. These people can literally astral travel while lying on their couch or using the bathroom. They have mastered the skill to the point where they do not have to be afraid of vising the astral planes. However, you are not at that level yet—even though you could be with regular practice. The point is that you shouldn't think of yourself as being completely immune and go without being prepared. Anything can happen in the astral plane; hence, the need to know what to expect. Below are ten things you need to know about astral projection and the astral plane before attempting an out-of-body experience.

1. Astral Projecting Can Be Dangerous

If you are wondering if astral projection can be dangerous, the answer is yes. Note that the keyword is "can," which means it has the potential of getting dangerous. Several beings and entities visit the astral plane. Not all of them are there to guide or help you; some will drain you of your auric energy and cause you harm. While this usually doesn't happen, you cannot rule out the possibility. But if you know how to shield and protect yourself using your vibration, nothing will happen to you. You cannot totally keep fear away when visiting the astral plane for the first time, but you can keep it at bay so that it doesn't overshadow the bright hue of your auric colors. Anyone with great psychic self-defense skills and the ability to keep their emotions at bay can safely navigate the astral plane. Astral projection is similar to traveling to another country on an airplane. It is normal to feel a sense of fear when you fly in an airplane for the first time, but you manage to keep the fear in check. You understand that nothing will happen as long as you follow the safety procedures of air travel. It is the same with astral projection and astral travel. Prepare yourself the right way, and you will easily have a safe astral experience, even as a beginner.

2. Astral Travel Is Real

Some people dabble in astral travel with a mindset of "fact-checking." They just want to know if astral travel is real or not. People who attempt an out-of-body experience to check if it is real, usually do not prepare for travel in the right ways. Doing something like this is akin to putting yourself in danger. Do not bother to attempt OBE if you are only bored. The mainstream media has deemed astral projection and astral travel as hoaxes. They dismiss both by saying that the astral body doesn't exist, or even if it does, it cannot leave the physical realm. Apparently, this defies the laws of physics. Scientific researchers believe that astral experiences are products of the mind—hallucinations, dreams, and figments of some memory seated deep within the subconscious mind.

Nevertheless, many controlled tests have shown that OBE is real and astral travel is, in fact, real. People who have successfully had out-of-body experiences have explained how it felt and what it seemed like. So many people cannot hallucinate the same things and have such similar experiences in the astral realm. So, yes, astral travel is *real*, and it works.

3. Anyone Can Learn Astral Travel

For some reason, many people believe that they need to be of a certain spiritual level before they can have an OBE. This is incorrect. Anybody can visit the astral plane and learn to do it regularly. The whole point of astral travel is to help you uncover the connection between your physical self and your spiritual essence. So, it doesn't matter whether you are already a spiritual person or are just trying it for the first time. One certain thing is that you may pick up on the techniques quickly or gradually, depending on how committed you are. That is normal. If you commit, you may learn to send your consciousness out of your physical form in just a fortnight. Some other people may spend months or even years before they finally learn to project their consciousness out of their bodies. The vital thing is to have the right mindset for learning astral projection. Even if you don't get it right instantly, keep believing that you will succeed. Doubt exists to limit people from unlocking their full potential. If you let doubt hold you back, you will never discover how far you can go. With patience and regular OBE practice, you will achieve your goal in time.

4. Location Matters

Before you attempt astral travel, ensure it is in a place where you feel secure. You cannot astral project your consciousness out of your physical form unless you can mentally relax and focus. To do this, you need to be in a location where there is a sense of security and safety. This helps your fear of what may happen to your physical body after you leave. If you are performing astral travel for the first time, it is best to do it in a place like your bedroom—somewhere you can come back to meet your physical body resting safely. If you attempt projection in a place where your feelings of fear and danger are heightened, you won't achieve anything. Remember that astral travel is both a spiritual experience and an educational one. You are doing it to learn about the things they don't teach you at college or in textbooks. Therefore, doing it the right way is vital.

5. Astral Travel Requires a Purpose

To travel the astral plane, you need a specific reason, purpose, or goal. What do you hope to achieve by performing astral travel? This is one question you should be able to answer wholeheartedly. If you cannot answer this question, do not bother engaging in astral travel. Most people say they want to astral travel, but they don't know why they want to. Astral travel is not for sightseeing; it is about learning, seeking answers, finding, and experiencing. Everything in the astral plane happens for a deeper reason. You learn something with every incident in the astral plane. The goal of astral travel is to help you evolve and grow within yourself, reaching a state of enlightenment that is impossible otherwise. Deep within your mind, you have a higher consciousness with knowledge about the true nature of existence. You are more connected with this consciousness in childhood, but as you grow older, you lose the connection you have with it. Astral travel is the key to connecting with the consciousness once more.

In some cases, astral travel is about healing. You may choose astral travel to find out the nature of an illness you are battling or as a means to heal yourself. The bottom line is that you should never try astral travel unless you have something you hope to achieve in mind, whether it is learning or healing.

6. Astral Travel Is Different from The Movies

Many movies have explored astral travel, but not many of them are right about the actual practice. In the Marvel superhero movie, *Doctor Strange*, the protagonists were constantly taking their astral forms to fight crime and the perpetrators of crime. In some movies, the protagonist ends up getting lost in the astral plane and can never return to their body. These are things that only happen in the movies and never in actual astral projection practice. In the astral plane, your soul automatically returns to your body when you experience any overwhelming emotions, such as fear or excitement. You automatically wake up in your body. It is your mind's way of protecting you, so it doesn't matter if the emotions you experience are positive. As long as that emotion is overwhelming, you will be returned to your physical form. Therefore, training yourself to keep your emotions in check while astral traveling is important. Be confident that you will never get lost forever, like the protagonists in the movies.

7. Meditation is Key to Astral Projection

If you want a smooth astral travel experience as a beginner, meditation is the way to go. It is not that meditation is a must, but it surely helps. There is no better way to have a proper experience than to meditate before astral projection. Conscious astral projection is different from lucid dreaming or unconscious astral travel in your dreams. Consciously going to the astral plane means experiencing something is real from an independent perception. Your mind normally cannot achieve this, because many things are holding it down. Meditating before astral projection or travel is the key to freeing the mind of the things holding it down. Meditation gets rid of all limiting and unnecessary thoughts. When you meditate for astral travel, your mind is focused on nothing but the experience you are about to have. You may not be able to pick this up on your first few tries—sometimes, you need hours and weeks of meditating before you can even achieve the most basic thing in astral travel. Meditation is also key to prolonging your stay in the astral plane. When you go to the astral plane in your astral form, your mind remains connected to your physical body, which explains why you can get pulled back when you experience a surge of emotions. Meditating before your project can help your mind stay calm and allow you to stay relaxed in the face of danger. Therefore, meditation can help prolong your out-of-body experiences.

8. Your Astral Form Can Do Anything Your Physical Form Does

Being in astral form has no limitation. It does not hold your back from doing certain things. In your astral form, you can even spy on others without them seeing you. Unless you go around clairvoyant or highly intuitive people, they likely won't see or feel you. However, this doesn't make it okay to go around disrespecting people's privacy. It may be difficult to do things such as spying while you are in the astral form, though. The purpose of astral projection is to enlighten and educate you, and your astral body will usually want to stay true to that purpose.

When you are out of your body, the astral plane is not the only place you can go. You may choose to stay on the prime material plane where you can watch your loved ones, fly to your best friend's house, or maybe just hang out on your street. You can also move up to a higher plane where you can meet your spirit guides or angels and chat with them about existence, reality, and anything that expands your awareness. Other planes may not align with your vibrating frequency. Going to these planes is akin to putting yourself at risk. It is not recommended that you go there without a powerful spiritual guide.

If you are over eighteen years of age, you may be interested in the chapter that discusses sex in the astral realm. Yes, you can do that too. Just be careful whom you do it with.

Now that you know everything you need to before attempting astral travel, it is time to prepare for your astral projection experiences.

Chapter Six: Preparing for Astral Projection

Traveling to the astral plane may be difficult, but it is not impossible. Many people have given up after several unsuccessful attempts to have an out-of-body experience. One of the problems is that very few resources have detailed steps on what you really need to do to prepare for astral projection. Hence, the struggle and difficulty. The one thing that may give you a hard time and make your OBE attempts unsuccessful is improper mental conditioning. If you do not prepare your mind properly for the experience, the chances of succeeding will be very low. The subconscious mind needs to be conditioned to prepare it for such an experience. More importantly, you have to get rid of the fears, anxiety, and anything else that may be bogging your mind down. While mentally conditioning yourself for the experience, you must also take enough time to practice before you finally make an actual attempt. Of course, it is okay if you don't get it right on the first try or the second or the third. The idea is to keep practicing until the astral realm opens itself up to you.

The most important thing you should do to prepare yourself for astral travel is to overcome any fear of the experience. You may be afraid that you will encounter some danger in your travel to the astral plane—that is okay. The key is not to let that fear overwhelm your mind to a crippling point. Some people may tell you that you have to get rid of fear completely before you can astral travel—that's impossible, especially if this is your first time and you fear the experience. You are bound to be scared. However, don't be scared to the point where you let fear overwhelm you. You can easily reduce your fear by expanding your knowledge of astral projection and familiarizing yourself with certain essential things that should be basic knowledge for anyone hoping to astral project.

While studying and enhancing your knowledge, set aside some daily time to practice positive affirmations, visualization, hypnosis, and other preparation techniques.

Positive Affirmations

Affirmations are powerful and effective tools for conditioning or reconditioning the mind. They should be an integral part of your daily activities when you are preparing for astral projection. Affirmations can also help you overcome your fear much faster. Some of the positive affirmations you can use include:

"I'm not afraid. Fear has no power over me."

"I will visit the astral plane."

"My consciousness will leave my body to take my astral form."

"I will have an out-of-body experience."

Whatever phrase you decide to use, make sure you keep them positive and purposeful. Be clear about what you will do, not what you want to do. For example, do not say, "I want to astral project." Say, "I will astral project." The purpose of positive affirmations is to reinforce your wish and goal in your subconscious. The more you practice, the readier your mind will be. Take note not to use phrases with negative connotations, especially those that connote fear or anxiety. Your mind can't distinguish between positive and negative affirmations; it can only reinforce anything you say. Use positive affirmations for everyday practice. Don't just use them whenever you are trying to project. Let it become a habit. Use them before and after you go to bed each night. This is when you are closest to your subconscious state. Keep reminding yourself of your reason for astral projection every time you practice.

Visualization

Visualization is another way you can prepare yourself for astral travel. Yet, most people seem to overlook its importance. Practicing visualization to prepare yourself for the astral plane should not be an option; it should be a core part of your attempts, successful or not. Thankfully, visualization is something you can practice several times a day, in different ways—and the more you practice, the better your chances of success. If you are the type who practices mindfulness meditation regularly, it should be easy for you. Visualization practice involves imagining things. In your case, it may be imagining that you are flying or floating—since this is the sensation people who have had OBEs usually describe. So, imagine that you are flying or floating—add as many details as possible as this is quite important.

If you are flying:

Choose how fast you are going—are you flying at the speed of a bird or an airplane? Where are you flying to? As you are flying, what can you see around you? Is it morning or night? Are there birds flying with you in the sky? Are there any sounds or smells? Does the wind feel warm or chilly on your face? Is the air blowing through your hair—if so, how does it feel?

These are the details you should put into your imagination. Do not be vague when you visualize; add every minor or big detail that comes to mind. Whatever you choose, immerse yourself completely into the imagination.

Another way you can use visualization is to imagine having astral sensations. Close your eyes and visualize you touching yourself—don't imagine anything sexual, as this may affect your projection techniques.

- Imagine using your hands to rub around your arm, shoulder, or knee in circular motions. You are doing this very gently.

- If you have to, touch yourself to make it feel real. Focus on the feel of your hand against your arm or knee. At the same time, focus on how your knee feels against your hand.

- Concentrate on the sensations and use your mind to recreate them. You may not get it immediately, but you will as long as you stay focused. The more you focus, the easier and more effective it becomes.

You can also imagine actual places that you have never been to before. It may be the landscape on your Windows desktop, a picture, or the art on your wall. Take a good look at it. Look at all the details, including the minutest ones. Take in the colors, shadows, textures—everything. Memorize the picture or painting. Next, go away from the object and try to recall everything you memorized. Do this every day, and soon, you will be able to use this method to achieve a projection. However, right now, just take it as a technique to condition your mind and ready it for projection.

Hypnosis and Subliminal Suggestions

Hypnosis is another incredibly effective technique for conditioning your mind for astral projection and out-of-body experiences. Do not be surprised if hypnosis ends up being more effective for you than all the previously discussed techniques. This is because hypnosis is a way to enter deep into your subconscious mind and prepare it for the experience. Positive affirmations and visualization are both ways of stopping your mind from letting fear and any other emotion overwhelm it. You don't want fear and doubt to cripple your mind and make you fail before you have even tried. Hypnosis and subliminal suggestion are more effective because you can include some of the other methods when you try hypnosis. However, you need the presence of a trained hypnotherapist if you want to use this method.

Tips for Getting Ready

Now, as well as the methods above, you must do one other thing to prepare yourself for astral travel. If you are trying to start an OBE session and attempt a projection, how do you get ready? Below are five tips that give insight into what to do right before attempting projection.

1. *DND - Do Not Disturb*

Just like you would not want to be disturbed when meditating, you cannot be disturbed during astral projection practice. So, find a quiet room where you can conduct your session without being disturbed by your partner, kids, pets, or anything. If you don't, your attempts may be ruined by these. For example, you may feel like you are finally getting it right, and then a call will come in and ruin the moment. Keep your mobile phone and media gadgets away from the room you want to use for practice. If you feel like you can't completely avoid being disturbed, it is best to practice at a time when everybody else is asleep. For instance, you can practice very early in the morning or at night when everyone is in bed. Your schedule will determine the time you choose. Just make sure it is an hour where you have your "me time."

2. *Make Yourself Comfortable*

Relax your mind. Get comfortable. Use some of the methods above to still your mind and get it ready. You may choose to lie in your bed or the couch. It is all up to you. Just make sure your posture is one that will allow you to stay motionless for as long as needed. Also, wear something light. If you want, you may decide to practice naked. If you would rather lay in bed, keep a light blanket around you or don't, depending on your weather. If you want to sit, it is best to use a reclining chair to help you remain comfortable during the whole session.

3. *Don't Set Time Limits*

Being time conscious can ruin your experience. Rather than see astral projection as something you need to do within a certain period, eliminate the time limits. Do not think of it as a race because it is not. Be free with yourself. Take as much time you need. Placing a time limit is one of the things that can inhibit your mind, just like fear. Eliminate the time concern and open yourself up to the experience.

4. *Choose the Right Timing*

Timing is the deciding factor for success. Think carefully about the right time to practice. While nighttime may seem ideal—since everyone else would be asleep—fatigue and stress may pose a problem, especially if you worked all day. Morning is better for many people; in fact, practicing straight after sleep increases your chances of success by a wide margin. Night attempts are usually harder. So, better to make your attempts in the morning.

5. *Be*

Yes, just be. Once you get your mind and body to relax, simply remain. Do not concern yourself with anything. Be, and allow your mind to conceive the images and everything else it wants until they fade and dissipate. Eventually, your mind will calm down, and you will be ready to project. Before attempting projection, though, perform a meditation exercise to get yourself in the right mental state.

Once you can successfully pull off the preparation stage, you are one step closer to having an out-of-body experience and visiting the astral plane. All you need to do now is try projecting.

Note: Before you attempt projection, ensure you have equipped yourself with astral protection tips. The astral plane is an unknown dimension; it is different from the physical plane. You will come across very strange things, but that should not alarm you. The right thing to do is to protect yourself before you go there. Some of the best ways to protect yourself are to wear a protective amulet or call on your spirit guides to protect you. More on that is discussed later.

Chapter Seven: 5 Basic Astral Projection Techniques

Projecting yourself into the astral plane is not the same as falling asleep, even though you can achieve it while in a sleep state. Sleeping is easy. A day of work can serve as your bedrock for a good, sound sleep. However, when it comes to astral traveling, you need more than just being tired. In fact, tiredness and fatigue will likely make your attempt fail rather than succeed. To astral travel, you need to propel yourself to a state where your body is asleep while your mind remains awake and alert. Then, you need to transit your consciousness into an astral vehicle, also known as your astral body. Everything else that happens in astral projection or travel is only possible after you accomplish the above. Although some basic things separate them, dreaming is a form of astral projection—an unconscious form. The soul sometimes leaves the body when you sleep. But you do not know this, so you can't control what it does when it leaves. In this case, your subconscious is in charge. The key difference between sleeping normally and astral projecting is that you are in charge of your soul when you astral project. In other words, you can consciously dictate where your soul goes, and you are aware of the experience. Conscious astral projection is what benefits you. So, what are some of the best techniques that will help you accomplish astral travel fast?

First, you should know that your success can be fast. You can learn to astral project in just a fortnight. Everything depends on you. Yes, there are tips and techniques to help you, but how committed are you willing to be? Do you even take astral travel seriously? Are you able to still your mind and kill your fears about the experience? All these are things that will impact your level of success. If you follow the tips in this book from the very basic to the more advanced, you will start astral traveling regularly. So, it is really up to you.

You should also know that there are tons of techniques that can be used to propel your consciousness out of your body. Every human is unique. A successful OBE technique for someone may not work for you. This is why there are more than five different techniques here to help you. If you try one for a while and it does not help you, move on to the next one. Try the techniques until you find one that works for you perfectly. In specific cases, some people only have to try one technique for the first time before finding out it's the perfect fit for them. Certain techniques are further superior to others, so the techniques below are some of the best ones that work for most people.

Rope Technique

If you have ever tried to learn about astral projection, you may have heard about this technique as it is quite popular. The rope technique is one of the most effective astral projection techniques. It was introduced by Robert Bruce and involves visualizing an imaginary rope hanging from the sky, your ceiling, or any surface above you. This rope is what you will then use to propel your astral body from the physical—you do this by putting pressure on a single point on your body. Before you start inducing astral projection, do not forget to prepare your mental state for the experience. It is best to practice this technique lying down.

- *Relax your body and mind.* Free your mind of all worry and stress. Lay down in a comfortable posture. Try tensing and releasing your muscles for some seconds to rid them of any tension. Once you are calm and relaxed, you can proceed.

- *Move your body to sleep.* Let your body feel numb and relax as deeply as possible, but not to the point where you lose consciousness. Don't try to stay awake; let your physical body go to sleep by inducing a sleep state. The simplest way to do this to lay on your bed or couch, close your eyes, and allow your thoughts to drift away. When you start losing physical sensations, it means your body is now moving toward sleep.

- *Lay down.* Do nothing. If you think that there is nothing much about this, you are partly right. It should feel like nothing is happening. Just remain still and do not move any part of your body. To enhance the near-sleep feeling, concentrate on the darkness in front of your closed eyes; you may experience some strange things while you are in this state. Don't fret—your field of vision will give a sensation of expanding. It may feel odd, but you will like the sensation. You may also become aware of some sounds and light patterns. Ignore these as they will fade away eventually. At this point, you should start to feel like you are floating or falling, without feeling or sensing anything. Maintain this state and feeling.

- *The vibration state.* This is a state that you will enter once you have induced your body to a state of sleep. While it doesn't exactly feel like vibrations, it is an effect that you will experience. It feels like being weightless and floating. By supercharging your willpower, you can increase the feeling and sensation—you can decrease as well. This feeling isn't something that can be accurately described. Wait until you experience it.

Reaching the vibration state is a milestone. If you can reach it on your first try, know that you are doing something right as not many people can reach this state. Keep in mind that you should maintain the vibration state for a while before you move on.

This state is a good time to explore deep within your mind and maybe even use a visualization method to inform yourself and have a deep introspection.

- *Imagine the rope.* Visualize a rope hanging from the surface above you, with the tip dangling a few inches from your face. Concentrate on this stage and put as many details as possible. Visualize the texture, weight, and movement of the rope. Does it feel rough or smooth? Light or heavy? Is it still or swaying with the breeze?

- *Touch the rope.* When you have successfully imagined the rope and clearly see it, imagine yourself reaching out and grasping it. If it is your first time, simply grasp the rope—don't do anything else. You should be able to feel the roughness or smoothness of the rope on your visualized hand. Then, try the second hand. By doing this, you are attempting to separate your limb from your physical form.

Now, visualize your second hand reaching up to grasp the rope very tightly. Stay in that position for a few seconds. Then, use your willpower and visualize, pulling your body up and out of your physical body. This may sound difficult, but you will find it easy when you start the actual practice.

If you accomplish pulling your astral from your physical form, that is it. Once you are out of your body, you can start floating to get the full experience. If you fall asleep while practicing, do not beat yourself up about it—just try again the next day. Don't let your first unsuccessful experience make you feel like a failure.

OBE from Lucid Dreaming

This technique involves transitioning from lucid dreaming to an out-of-body experience. As you already know, lucid dreaming is the kind of dream where you dream while remaining fully conscious and aware of the experience—and you also remain in command of your dream. Lucid dreaming and astral projection are two different things, but lucid dreaming can be used as a prop for achieving astral projection. To learn how to transition from lucid dreaming to astral projection, you must first know how to achieve a lucid state while dreaming. When you enter a lucid dreaming state, your consciousness leaves your body to a place conceived by your subconscious mind. Now what you have to do is induce a lucid dreaming state and then transfer your consciousness from that imaginary place to your bedroom.

- *Think of OBEs.* Read about OBEs. Let the thought of having an out-of-body experience stay in your mind all day. The goal here is to besot your mind with thoughts of OBEs. This technique is best practiced at night, so think about OBEs during the day.

- *Use positive affirmations to trigger your mind so it can induce a lucid dreaming state.* During the day, say things like, "I'm going to have a lucid dream and transition to the astral plane." Keep reminding yourself of this all day. And, most importantly, occasionally remember to ask yourself, "Am I dreaming right now?" Within a few days, you will have successfully reconditioned your mind to induce a lucid dreaming state while you are asleep. The next step is to wait.

- *Post-lucid dreaming.* When you finally have a lucid dream and are aware of it, immediately imagine that you are dreaming and not in your body. Try this, and you should feel your consciousness go free and become independent of your physical form. Another thing you should note is that lucid dreaming will take place in any dreamland your subconscious recreates. So, use your willpower and will yourself to be in your bedroom instead.

As soon as you do this, you should find yourself floating in your bedroom, with your physical body lying restfully on the bed.

Just like that, you have accomplished your goal of astral projection. Before you use this method, make sure you practice ordinary lucid dreaming first. Once you start inducing a lucid dreaming state without a hitch, you can proceed to astral projection and astral travel.

Displaced-Awareness Technique

The point of this technique is to displace your sense of awareness and direction so that you end up in the astral plane. To use this technique, you have to enter a trance-like state and use visualization to displace yourself. Many people find this technique incredibly easy to execute, and the attempts are mostly always successful.

• *Close your eyes.* Enter a trance-like state as described in the first technique—relax until your body is as still as possible. Then, visualize the room your session is in. Try to absorb the sensation of the whole room all at once by projecting it into your consciousness. This means that you should literally be able to view the room exactly as it is in your mind.

• *Be as passive as possible about the experience.* Imagine the feeling of you watching the entire room above your shoulders.

• *Visualize your astral body.* Imagine it rotating slowly and gently at 180 degrees. Once you finish the rotation in your mind, your astral head should be positioned where you have your physical feet, and your astral feet should be where you have your physical head. This means that your astral and physical bodies should be directly opposite each other. With this image in your head, try imagining your room in this new direction. The idea here is to get your subconscious mind to forget where you really are and displace your sense of direction. If you do this the right way, you will get a sudden feeling of dizziness. Don't be scared as this is normal. Remain in that state for some minutes until you feel comfortable.

- *Floating*. Once you are comfortable in that state, the next stage is to visualize yourself floating toward the surface above you, i.e., your ceiling or roof. Let this feel as real as possible. Don't be surprised to find your astral form suddenly pop out of your physical form.

As simple as this technique seems, it is easier to sleep off while practicing. You should practice this technique after waking up from sleep as your mind and body will be naturally rested and relaxed after a good sleep. Keep in mind that you do not have to get it right on your first try. This technique needs time to perfect. So, make practice an ongoing thing and be patient. You will be surprised at the results when you finally perfect this technique.

Watching yourself Sleep

This technique is similar to the second technique. You need to induce a trance-like state for your physical body to propel your astral form from it. Start this technique in the morning when you are still drowsy, and your body can easily go back to sleep. This is key to reaching the relaxation and awareness level that you need to pull this technique off.

- *Lie down on your couch, bed, or any flat surface that is comfortable to practice in.* Relax your muscles by loosening the tension and knots you feel in them. Close your eyes. Try to rid your mind of distracting thoughts by focusing on the feel of your body. Do not leave this stage until you have achieved a complete state of mind and body relaxation.

- *Help yourself enter a state of hypnosis.* The hypnotic state is referred to as the hypnagogic state. Lure your body to sleep without allowing yourself to lose consciousness. Hypnosis is like being at the edge of the bridge between wakefulness and sleep. Until you achieve this state, the astral projection will not be possible.

- *Enter a hypnotic state.* To do this, close your eyes firmly but without forcing it or exerting pressure on your eye muscles. Allow your mind to concentrate on any specific part of your body, such as your foot or finger. Focus on the body part until it starts to take form in your mind even as your eyes are closed. Keep your focus on it until all other thoughts drift away. Using your mind, twitch your finger gently—don't move it physically. Visualize the finger twitching or curling until you can feel it like it's happening physically.

- *Move the focus to other parts of your body.* This includes your head, legs, arms, and hands. Move each part using your mind. Remain steady until you can mentally move your whole body.

- *Enter the state of vibration as described in the first technique.* The vibrating sensations may come in waves or gently. They usually arrive when your soul is about to depart your physical body for the astral form. Keep any feelings of fear in check to avoid disrupting your meditative state. Lose yourself to the vibrations.

- *Using your mind, propel your consciousness from your body.* Visualize the room you are in. Will yourself to stand up with your mind. Look around and get off the bed. Then, walk around your room and look back at your physical form.

- *The astral state.* If you feel a sensation of looking down at your own body from another perspective, you have successfully entered the astral state, and your consciousness is now independent of your body. This stage understandably requires tons of practice for some people. If you are one of them, keep practicing. If moving your whole body seems too difficult, try a leg or hand at first. Then, gradually build up to your whole body.

If you have sharp intuitive abilities, the vibration state may come as easily as breathing to you. However, even if you do not, it will still come if you keep practicing. Once your astral form is in travel mode, you can float up to the astral realm.

The Monroe Technique

Dr. Monroe is one of the pioneers of astral projection in the mainstream media. You have likely heard about the Monroe technique if you have already dabbled in astral projection and OBEs. His technique is an incredibly simple and straightforward one, similar to the rope technique with just a few differences. The Monroe technique is more than likely to help you reach an astral state if you have the right tips. Below are seven simple steps to follow it effectively.

1. *Relax.* This is required for all techniques as it induces an out-of-body experience. Relax your body and mind with any relaxation technique discussed so far.

2. *After entering a relaxed state, proceed to induce a hypnogogic state.* Lure yourself to sleep without letting your consciousness fall asleep. You can use the method in the previous technique to induce a hypnogogic state.

3. *When you feel yourself reaching the near-sleep state, go deeper to reach conditions.* Condition A is when you are finally in a near-sleep state. From condition A, move to condition B—a deeper relaxative state where you notice the light and sound patterns. From condition B, move to condition C—an even deeper state than B. By the time you reach condition C, you would have lost complete awareness of all sensory stimulation in your physical body. But your mind will be there to serve as your only stimulation. You are now in a state of emptiness. Before you project, you have to ensure you reach condition D.

4. *After reaching condition D, you have to enter into a vibratory state.* This is the state right before you project your soul out of your physical body.

5. *Control your vibratory state by visualizing waves of vibrations in every part of your body.* The best way to do this is to focus on the tingling sensations caused by the vibratory state and extending the sensation from one part of your body to the next. To initiate projection successfully, you must take full charge of the vibratory state.

6. *Attempt a partial separation from your body.* Focus your thoughts on detaching from your body. Make sure you don't lose track of your thoughts, as this might make you lose the vibratory state. Gently propel a part of your astral form from your body—you may choose a foot or your hand. Extend it from your physical body and attempt to touch something close to you. Allow your hand or foot to go through the item you touch and then retract it to your physical form. If you do this successfully, you can progress to a full-blown projection.

7. *You can now detach completely from your physical body.* There are two ways you can do that, according to this technique. Firstly, imagine that you are getting lighter and floating upwards. Remain focused, and you will feel your consciousness go out of your body. Or, you can use the rotation technique that involves rolling over—the same way you do when you get out of bed. Be careful not to move your body physically. Before you know it, you will find yourself lying separately from your physical body. Now, all you need to do is imagine yourself floating upwards while looking down at your physical body.

Try all that, and you will have a successful astral projection by the last stage.

Muldoon's Thirst Technique

This technique is not generally recommended for beginners, because it is somewhat unpleasant. However, it's just as effective as every other technique on this list. Muldoon's thirst technique involves not drinking water throughout the day and then using thirst as a driving sensation to induce an out-of-body experience. You see a glass of water and imagine yourself drinking it. You do this every few hours throughout the whole day. Then, before you sleep, you place a glass or cup a few feet from your bed and lick a pinch of salt. At this point, you should be really thirsty, but still don't drink it. Just lay in bed and keep visualizing yourself reaching out for the glass of water or walking over to the water and drinking it. By luck, your astral form will eventually pull out of your body to get the glass of water and drink. You can then seize that opportunity to explore the material plane or go higher up into the astral plane.

Other Basic Astral Projection Techniques

There are other astral projection techniques that you can use to achieve an out-of-body state. They include:

• *The jump technique.* This is a very simple astral projection technique that involves giving yourself a reality check. Basically, you ask yourself if you are dreaming. Ask seriously and sincerely, wait for an answer, and then jump. In a waking state, you will merely rise and land. However, in a dreaming state, you will feel your astral state take off and fly away when you jump.

• *The stretching technique.* Lie down. Relax. Imagine your feet stretching and expanding until it is one or more inches longer. Once you can maintain this image firmly in your mind, return your feet to its normal size. Repeat this process with your head. Go back and forth between your feet and head, stretching them longer at each try. When you stretch beyond two feet, try doing both at once. Soon, you will have dizzying sensations and feel vibrations. Then, you can float from your room.

• *The hammock technique.* Visualize yourself sitting in a bright-colored hammock between two or more palm trees on a beach where you are alone. Feel the breeze on your face and visualize the wind swaying you. Maintain this image in your head until you feel yourself swaying out of your still body. Finally, roll out from your body to the site and float upwards to start your exploration.

Regardless of the astral projection technique you use, the chances of you succeeding on your first try are very low. You may try for several weeks before you finally start seeing a tangible result. Even if you cannot project immediately, know that every step you accomplish is a win for you. If you reach the hypnogogic state on your first try, that counts as a massive accomplishment, and you should treat it as such. On your next try, if you enter the vibratory state successfully, that also counts. It shows that you are doing something right, and you will be astral projecting in no time. Just take your time and remain relaxed at all times. Do not make it feel like a race or something you need to achieve within a specific timeframe.

The great thing about astral projection is that your sense of awareness expands with each try, regardless of failed or successful attempts. Every practice session is an opportunity to enhance your sense of awareness and strengthen your auric field.

Chapter Eight: Advanced OBE Techniques

The advanced OBE techniques are various techniques that use skills such as visualization, affirmations, hypnosis, dream transition, and sound. The techniques require these skills so that you can find one that really suits you. If you have poor visualization skills, you can use the affirmation techniques or dream transition. However, visualization techniques are some of the most popular OBE techniques. As you can see, most of the basic OBE techniques are visualization-based. After choosing a specific technique, keep practicing with it for at least thirty days. The results you achieve will depend on your commitment and the effort you put into practice. Keep in mind that the best approach to using any of these techniques is to assume a playful and lighthearted demeanor. Do not feel like you are about to do something severe. Free your mind so that you can have fun and enjoy any result you achieve.

Target Technique

This is a visualization technique that engages one or more of your five senses. The targeting technique involves focusing attention on an object outside of your physical body and using that to lull yourself into the hypnogogic state. You may choose a place, object, or person to focus on as long as it is not a part of you. The object or person you choose has to be some distance away. It could be your favorite diner or your ex-partner. It can also be an object that holds special meaning to you. Whatever it is, it should be a physical and tangible object—something you can set your eyes on. You cannot use an imaginary place or person for this technique. Choose an object or place that you feel the closest to. Many people find visualizing a loved one, whom they are separated from, effective. Do not choose someone you have never had an emotional connection with, like a celebrity crush.

Visualize yourself and this person together. Breathe in their presence and allow yourself to feel absorbed to the point where it feels like you are actually together. If you wish, you can start some form of interaction to keep you engaged in their presence. Maintain the visual creation in your mind for as long as possible as you let your body relax and start to drift off to sleep. It is essential to add as many details as possible to your visualization, including the interaction you are having with this person. As your physical body dozes off to sleep, your mind should remain alert and awake. This method is excellent for bedtime visualization practice as it hastens your transition into the hypnogogic state. Remember, the more involved you are with your target, the better this method will work. So, allow your imagination to run wild if that is what helps. Maintaining focus and awareness using this technique is greatly enhanced when you direct your attention entirely upon a chosen object or place that is near.

This exercise is one that works effectively for developing this ability.

- Choose three targets in your home. The three targets should be tangible items that you can envision easily. All three should be in another part of your home, away from the room where you practice this out-of-body technique. For example, the first target could be your favorite sofa. The second target could be your prom dress from high school. For the third target, it could be visually stimulating, such as the vase you got from your vacation in Japan. Ensure these three targets are all in one room.

• After choosing your targets, walk to the room where you have the targets in your physical body. Scrutinize each one and take in every detail with meticulous ease. Study them one by one from different views. Note if there are any irregularities or imperfections. Take your time to assimilate the look and feel associated with each target.

• Tune in to your five senses as you walk to each object to thoroughly examine it, but focus more on sight and touch. How does each object feel and look? Walk to the room several times until you can remember each target's most basic details, including the weight, textures, colors, and densities. Also, take note of the sensations that accompany your walk from one object to the other.

This technique aims to help you maintain awareness while keeping the focus away from your physical body. As you concentrate fully on the targets, your physical body will start to drift off to sleep. If you remain persistent, you will get dramatic results. To heighten this method's sensations, use a whole month just to repeat the visual and physical walk-through. You only need thirty minutes for each practice. Make sure you select targets that you can easily visualize when the time comes. This technique will get you in the hypnogogic state faster than some of the other techniques. It is handy. Once you enter the hypnogogic state, follow the other steps in Chapter Seven.

Sound Frequency Technique

The Tibetan shamans have been using sounds to induce out-of-body experiences for years. They use chants, bells, and chimes to heighten their meditative state. It has been proven that repetitive sounds can be useful in improving focus and awareness in humans. This sound frequency technique is a method that has been used by monks for centuries. It is a classic technique and is quite straightforward.

- Breathe in and out very deeply and allow your body to relax completely. Make yourself feel comfortable in your chosen OBE spot. Close your eyes and concentrate just above your crown chakra. Focus all of your awareness there until you start to lose sensations in your body.

- As your sensations fade from your physical body, gently intone *OM* seven times. Make sure the sound resonates through the top of your head.

- Intone the *OM* sound again seven times. Pay attention to the sound's resonation in your mind; allow it to go to the crown of your head.

- Concentrate on the very point of the resonating sounds and allow the sound to gradually shift through the ceiling, ascending to the surface above. Feel your awareness mesh with the sound to become one. Become a part of the sound and let it become a part of you. As your body relaxes and falls off to a dreamlike state, merge with the rising sound.

- Feel your awareness rise with the sound. Enjoy the sound and let it flow through you—as though you are one. Allow your body to relax and sleep as your mind concentrates on the *OM* sound. Do not take attention away from the sound until your physical body falls asleep, and you feel the astral plane open up to you.

This out-of-body technique works more effectively when you pair it with an OBE induction sound tape.

Higher Self Connection Technique

OBEs and astral travel's ultimate goal is to help you become closer with your spiritual essence, your higher self. Only when you align with your higher self will you reach a state of ultimate enlightenment and awareness. When you are connected with your higher self, entering the astral plane for an out-of-body experience becomes much more comfortable. The following steps will help you get in touch with your higher self.

- *Sit comfortably and close your eyes.* Focusing on the sensation and rhythm of your breath, allow all of your thoughts to dissipate slowly. Keep concentrating on your breathing until all of your thoughts about today clear away.

- *Make a sincere request to your heart to grant you a visual symbol of your higher self.* Open your mind to all impressions that come. Do not pass judgments; just focus.

- *In your mind's eye, visualize that your higher self is coming from a distance toward you.* This may appear in any way that holds a significant meaning to you. Now, your higher self-symbol is in front of you. You can sense and feel its radiant glow of lights and the reverberating energy from around it. Take as much time as possible to envision, open yourself up to, and be with your higher self.

- *Clearly imagine yourself merging with the spiritual symbol to become one.* Surrender to its energy and light as nothing should restrict your connection to the higher self. Acknowledge that no separation exists between your conscious self and the higher self.

- *Let your thoughts drift off and merge with your intention to embody your higher self.* Allow all shifts within to occur as your awareness melds to become one with your powerful higher self.

An established connection with the higher self makes astral projection much easier. Additionally, regular OBE practice can help strengthen this connection once it is established.

The Mirror Technique

This is another visualization technique for inducing an out-of-body experience. It can significantly increase your visualization skills and prepare you for the exploration of the astral plane.

- Place a full-length mirror in your OBE practice room. The mirror should be in a location that allows you to see your total reflection without physically moving your body.

- Look into the mirror and study your image. Examine and reflect on the image before you and start memorizing it. Try to be as objective and detached as possible. Think of your reflection as an object you want to paint in your head. Take in even the minutest details. Pay attention to the fit of your clothes and body. Take as much time as you need to memorize every feature you see.

- Now, close your eyes and start visualizing yourself in as many details as you can remember. Repeat this process until you can mentally visualize yourself on the opposite side of your room.

- Keep your eyes closed and envision yourself standing on the other side of your room. Then, start picturing the visualized image of yourself moving from one part of the room to another.

- Next, visualize your imaginary self slowly moving your fingers and hands, before slowly moving your whole arm. Envision your reflection moving its feet and legs. To whatever extent you can, allow yourself to become emotionally and mentally involved in your reflection's actions.

- Note as you start experiencing the sensations of these movements. Enjoy as you feel the sensations without your physical body. Immerse yourself in the movements, and the sensations they are producing.

- As you immerse yourself, visualize yourself, stand up slowly, and walk across the room. As you walk, pay attention to the sensations that accompany your movements.

- Feel yourself opening your imaginary eyes from the reflection. With as much clarity as you can muster, picture your reflection looking around the room. This should feel like you are watching the room from a new perspective, and that is okay. Just go with it. The more you practice this technique, the stronger your ability to view the world from beyond the physical form's limits.

- One by one, start transferring your senses—from sight to touch—to the image walking around your room. As most of your perception skills move to the imaginary self, lose all awareness of your physical body. Entirely focus on your imaginary self with the new sensations and sight.

- Relax and allow your physical body to fall asleep. As your body gradually drifts off to sleep, you will feel a shift of your consciousness from your physical to the astral body. Make sure you remain calm as this happens.

The mirror technique is entirely based on visualization. It remains one of the fastest techniques for inducing an out-of-body experience. It is easy to learn and even more comfortable to practice. With consistency and effort, the mirror technique will help you learn astral projection. But more importantly, you can significantly improve your visualization skills for other purposes with the mirror technique for out-of-body experiences. Make sure to enjoy the whole thing as you practice.

REM Technique

This is called the REM technique because you can only do it in the early morning after two REM sessions have passed. When you are asleep, during every 90 to 100 minutes, you enter a dream session known as the Random Eye Movement or REM. During this period, the eye movement is the physical proof that you are entering a dream or any other state in which awareness is altered. Science is yet to establish a connection between out-of-body experiences and REM. Still, there is no doubt that the two are linked somehow. The REM technique requires a high level of self-discipline, but it is quite useful and secure.

• Set your alarm for three hours of sleep. Once it rings and you awaken, go to your usual OBE practice room.

• Make yourself comfortable and use any of the astral projection techniques that have been discussed so far. Start repeating your affirmations verbally and then say them silently to yourself.

• As your body relaxes in this state, focus entirely on the affirmations and steer your mind away from your physical body. As you enter the hypnogogic state, try increasing the impact of your affirmations on your psyche. Increase the intensity of the affirmations. Make the last one firm, personal, and clear—it should trigger an instant out-of-body experience. Your last thought before your body drifts completely off to sleep should be your out-of-body affirmations.

Do not forget to focus all of your awareness on the affirmations. The intensity of the affirmations and the level of commitment you feel toward them are also very important. This method works for many people and is generally sufficient. If you do it right, you will induce an out-of-body experience immediately after your body goes to sleep.

These are some of the advanced astral projection techniques. They are generally easy to follow; however, you may need to sharpen your visualization skills before you attempt some of them. Regardless, it helps to start with the basic techniques. The basic astral projection techniques are straightforward, and they don't really require you to have powerful visualization abilities. In the end, it is your choice to make. If you like a challenge, feel free to go for the harder ones, such as the target technique.

Chapter Nine: What to Expect When Astral Projecting

Understanding what astral projection feels like takes actually experiencing it. Detaching your astral form from your physical body is also unique to each individual. You may not experience astral projection in the same way as someone else; however, there are some familiar sensations that everyone who has ever had an out-of-body experience usually reports. Knowing these sensations before your experience gives insight into what to expect when your soul leaves your body. Embracing the sensations can make your astral projection experience even more wholesome. As wholesome as these sensations are, they are often difficult to explain to people who have never felt them. But when you have the experience, you can fully assimilate the remarkability of astral projection. However, no matter how unfamiliar the sensations during your astral projection experience feel, you have to embrace them. Shying away from them out of fear will only result in failed astral travel attempts. Below are some of the familiar sensations you may experience in astral mode and how best to react to them.

Paralysis

Sleep paralysis happens to most people during astral travel and usually happens during the point of preparation for astral projection. Paralysis and stiffness occur due to the hypnogogic state where you stiffen your entire body and leave just your mind active. As a result, your physical body becomes paralyzed similarly to the paralysis state it enters when you are in sleep mode. If this happens, you do not have to be afraid as you can wake your body up if needed. If you are trying astral travel for the first time, you may be unprepared for the experience and feel uncomfortable if you cannot move your body. The best way to keep panic off your mind is to imagine your body falling slowly to sleep while your mind remains in a dreamlike state. In case you feel super uncomfortable—to the point where you can't continue to remain in the state—you only need to jar your body awake. Otherwise, you have to embrace the paralysis to proceed in your astral journey.

Vibrations

Vibrations are familiar with every OBE experience because you have to go through the vibrational state before separating your astral body from the physical one. The vibrations have been reported to feel like a jolt of electricity. However, the intensity may vary from individual to individual. While you may experience it minimally, someone else may feel as if their whole body is convulsing, or vice versa. The exciting thing is that the effect of the vibrations on your body cannot be visible to anybody watching. The vibrational state only becomes attainable when your energy centers—chakras—reach an aligned resonation. As the energy points become synchronized, it may feel like opening multiple portals at the same time. At that point, you can open up and project into the astral plane. Experienced astral projectors can induce the vibrational stage and increase or decrease the intensity at will. With practice, you may also reach this level of ability.

Increased Heart Rate

Astral projection can be quite intense, regardless of whether you are a beginner or experienced projector. The intensity of the experience is usually higher for beginners, which is why you may feel your pulse speeding at an insane rate. You may literally hear your heart beating in your ears. Think back to the first time you tried to work out and remember how out of breath you felt while running. So, when you lie still and feel yourself enter the dreamlike state, where the only active thing is your mind, do not be too surprised to feel your heart racing faster than usual. You need a lot of confidence and willpower to go through with an astral projection experience. Emotions such as anxiety and excitement may further contribute to your beating heart. This is because these emotions trigger the release of adrenaline, which will inadvertently increase your heart rate. Try not to focus on your racing heart; instead, work on focusing your mind on what really matters, which is the experience you are about to have.

Buzzing

The vibrational state comes with certain sounds that are quite distinctive and loud. These sounds may gradually seep into your consciousness or come as a sudden echo. Astral projectors mostly report hearing sounds when they enter the vibrational state. The sound may be faint and sweet to your ears, making them tingle. For another person, the sound may be loud and surrounding—similar to the sound you hear when flying on a private jet. You may also experience a *whooshing* sound, as though the air was blowing through your ears on a windy day. Other noises include a *roaring*, *popping*, or *rushing* sound. These sounds are essential because they get the astral world to open up to you much faster. Therefore, you can learn how to make them happen whenever you want to enter the astral plane. One of the most effective ways to do this is to listen to binaural beats.

Tingling/Numbness

Tingling is usually a part of every astral projector's out-of-body experience. However, in some cases, you may experience the exact opposite of tingling. The two sensations are two ends of a scale. If you react to the astral projection by becoming overly aware of sensations, your body will experience tingling in a mild or intense level. It may be a quick and gentle stinging sensation on your skin or an itchy feeling that makes you super uncomfortable. For some, it may feel like electricity jolting through the body at very high currents.

On the other hand, if you react by becoming under-sensitive to the sensations, your body becomes numb, and you cannot feel anything happening. You are just there, like in a paralyzed state. Numbness means that your conscious mind is the only thing awake and active.

Sinking

A sinking feeling is another prevalent sensation that most astral projectors report. You will likely feel a sort of pressure on your body. The feeling may be mild or tightening, depending on the intensity of the pressure. This sinking feeling is a result of your body feeling heavy and pressing downward. It is normal. It precedes the state right before projection. Increased activity in your crown chakra is responsible for the feeling of pressure. The sensation only lasts for a fleeting moment. So, what you can do is stay patient until it passes. Distract your mind from the feelings of discomfort that may accompany it. Just keep breathing and remain in the original tranquil state until your astral form separates from your physical body.

Floating

After your astral body has successfully separated from your physical self, you may feel yourself levitating. This is probably the most exhilarating part of astral projection—doing something that you only watch actors do in the movies. In the build-up to astral travel, you will experience a floating sensation. Basically, you feel your body being propelled from your bed to the surface above by some nonphysical force. That force is your mind. You may be able to control the speed at which you float and the length you reach, but this is unlikely on your first successful attempt. Unfortunately, some people unpleasantly experience this floating sensation. They feel their stomach drop to the ground due to the change in height. All these feelings are still possible to experience because you are still attached to your physical body. Once you separate from the physical body, all feelings associated with a physical form will fade away. Remember that the astral form is not held back by limitations, unlike the physical body. Therefore, physical disabilities are nonexistent in the astral form. Your astral body can explore the universe at will without being held back by physical inabilities or coming to physical harm. Your mind is the only limitation you have in the astral world, and it is up to you anyway.

Loud Noise

Apart from the *buzzing* sound you hear in your vibrational state, astral projectors have reported other sounds. If you have ears for music, you may be more sensitive to these sounds than others. Prepare yourself for the possible noise, so it does not interrupt your tranquil state. One thing about noises in the astral form is that they can get louder and louder, almost as if someone is in charge of the volume button. The sounds range from ring tones to bells ringing and even a hint of actual music. Don't panic if you happen to hear any of these noises. It is inevitable to experience sounds in the astral form. So, all you can do is to prepare your mind for the experience.

When you eventually astral project, you will likely feel at least one or more of these sensations. Since you now know what to expect, there should be no problem remaining in your relaxed state when the noises eventually happen.

3 Frequently Asked Questions about Travel in the Astral Plane

Three questions always come up in discussions about astral projection, and the answers to them help set up the right expectations. More importantly, they help assuage the fear that accompanies the thought of something as serious as astral travel.

"Can someone else take control of my body in the astral plane?"

If there is anything that the word "impossible" describes, it is this—your body cannot be occupied by any other spirit but yours. Astral projection, although slightly different, is almost the same as sleep. If another person can't take over your body while you sleep, it certainly won't happen in the astral plane. Your physical body isn't in any potential danger.

"Do I communicate with people on the astral plane?"

Of course, you can communicate with people on the astral plane—just be careful whom you talk to. There are different levels of existence on the astral plane. So, communication may depend on the plane you go to when you are in your astral form. You may meet people who are astral traveling in their dreams. Any attempt to communicate with these people will be futile as they are unconscious and preoccupied. The best thing to do is to mind your own business. Do not attempt to talk to people first. Even when they speak to you, make sure you assess the situation before you reply. The astral realm is a very vulnerable place, so it is best to avoid sharing your feelings and sentiments with the wrong entities.

"*What does the astral plane look like?*"

You cannot get a definitive answer to this. The astral plane does not take on one singular appearance to everybody. How it looks to you will depend largely on your auric field and the synchronization of your energy points. However, you will find that your environment will take on a new look once you project your astral form. For instance, your bedroom or practice room will take on a kind of astral look—which means it won't exactly look like your room.

Many more questions are asked about astral projection, but these three are the ones that are most relevant to your travel in the astral plane.

In the next chapter, find out how you can protect yourself from dangerous entities in the astral plane.

Chapter Ten: Protecting Yourself in the Astral Plane

Immaterial entities reside in the astral plane. Some of these entities do not even live there, but visit, just like you. While you will encounter nice and benevolent beings, such as angels and spirit guides, you will also come across malevolent ones. Hence, it is vital to be properly protected and armed during astral travel. Without proper protection tips or objects, you can come across a malicious spirit that will either trick you, scare you, or muddle up your mind. Spirits in the astral plane may not harm you physically; however, they can psychologically damage your energy core. The astral plane is a composition of different planes. Several entities and spirits reside in these planes. It is segregated into two: the lower astral plane and the higher astral plane.

The lower astral plane is the storehouse for all kinds of evil and everything humans fear. This is the first plane you will reach. Going to the higher parts of the astral realm requires you to pass through the lower plane, which is when you are most likely to encounter danger in any form. If your astral form is very powerful and carries an ever-shining light, malevolent spirits from the lower plane can still follow you into the higher realm. They simply have to follow the glow from your astral form.

You will find your deepest fears in the lower astral plane. Some of the entities that you see in the movies are real, and you can find them in the lower plane. From demons to ghosts to evil spirits, you will find most of the beings that make your spine shiver in the lower astral realm. This is not surprising as you already know that the lower astral realm is the repository for evil. The lower vibrational entities in the lower plane may follow you around to steal and harvest the light and energy from your astral form. It is like ants to sugar. It's even worse when you allow them to smell fear and uncertainty all over you. To keep you safe, here are five helpful tips that work for every astral projector.

Increase your Vibration

Entities in the lower astral plane are attracted to your fears and doubts more than anything. They are attracted to emotions that give off negative vibrational energy. Hence, raising your vibrations to as high a level as possible is an effective way of getting them to stay away from you. When your vibrations are at the highest level, lower level entities find it challenging to see or move toward you. More specifically, a higher vibration will also invite other higher vibrational beings to you, and you may interact with these entities. Regardless, increased vibrations mean your light will be glowing very brightly, which may continue to attract the lower vibration entities. So, be prepared despite the increased vibrations.

Avoid Trouble

Prevention will always be better than a cure for good reasons. One of the most effective ways to protect yourself from beings in the lower astral realm is to avoid having anything to do with them. So, if you can, evade lower-level entities entirely. In most cases, when you are preparing to visit the astral plane, your intuition gives you a hint of what may be awaiting you in the realm at that particular point. If your body feels like something is off, it is better to move the date to another day. Sometimes, though, you may not get any precognitive forewarning. However, when you reach the astral plane and sense a lower real entity coming to meet you or lying in wait for you, see if you can take another route or simply return to the material plane or your physical body. You can get in your body, wake, and wait for a while before attempting to go back to the astral plane. Do not go back unless you are sure that the being is gone. Normally, the immaterial entities don't remain in the same place for too long as they are always finding the next unsuspecting astral visitor to drain their energy.

If an entity is attracted to your light and starts heading in your direction, run. Go to another plane or the prime material plane. If you need to, go back to your physical body. Do not leave room for the entity to overtake you or catch up with you. The faster you can get out of its sight, the better for you. Once you speed up and leave plenty of ground for them to catch up, malicious spirits will most likely stop chasing. Then, you can continue on your journey.

Fight and Seek Help

If the above steps fail, you may have to fight any entity trying to absorb your light. A fight in the astral form is different from your usual physical fight. The fight here is to protect your mind, which is also the only thing you have as a weapon in the astral plane. With your mind, visualize and produce an armor of light around yourself. To take it up a notch, create an astral sword while you are at it. On the astral plane, an armor of light can only be created from within your own energy points, using the power of happiness, love, and compassion. It is meant to serve as your protective shield. To mentally conjure an armor of light, you have to concentrate on thoughts of love, happiness, and tranquility. At the same time, you must use positive affirmations to assure yourself that you are being covered in a shield of light. This is the same process you follow to create your own astral love. The key difference is that you have to draw from internal love to conjure a sword of light that is powerful enough to fight lower vibrational beings from the lower astral plane.

If any entity confronts or approaches you, do not be afraid to attack them. Get rid of fear and focus on your need for peace and calm. Should you stab the entity with your astral sword, they will feel the full impact of your love and eventually vanish or repel gradually. If they try to attack you, your astral form will be shielded by your armor of light, and you will be safe.

However, the spirits may sometimes catch you off guard, which means you may find it difficult to create the armor of light and your astral sword. In this case, your other option is to call out to higher vibrational entities to help you. Angels and spirit guides are readily available to help you when needed. They can assist in keeping malevolent spirits away. Since they are more familiar with the astral plane and know the entities they share the realm with, angels and spirit guides are more than likely to manage the situation better than you.

5 Things That Can Help You Increase your Vibration

Once you start regular astral projection practice, you will become more and more familiar with what vibrations are. Even if you cannot contextually understand what vibrations are, you will feel them every time you are in the astral plane. You need high levels of vibration to stay formidable in the astral realm. However, vibrations are not something you can just increase at will. To increase your vibrational level, you must have been practicing and putting in the work in your physical form too. Otherwise, you will not draw upon your vibrations as protection when the moment to protect yourself from a mean spirit in the astral plane arrives. To prepare your mind and body for a wholesome astral experience, below are tips to help you increase your vibrations in the physical and astral planes.

1. *Be grateful.* Gratitude is a very important emotion that most people unfortunately underrate. Being grateful is one of the fastest ways you can enhance your vibration. Plus, it is something you can do immediately—even while reading this book. Look around you and find something you are thankful for. This might seem like a hard thing, but you would be surprised to find just how many things you can be grateful for in a single moment. From your breathing to the shelter or the bed you are in, be grateful for something that matters. Look at the beautiful clouds and be grateful for them. Gratitude is a high-energy emotion, which is why it can serve as a source for increasing your vibration. Whenever you feel yourself experiencing a low-level emotion, simply shift your focus away from this emotion by finding something to be thankful for. Make gratitude your habit, and your sense of spiritual awareness may start to expand.

2. *Love.* Think about someone in your life who is easy to love. Visualize that person sitting with you and see how it makes you feel. When you think about them, a feeling of lightness and happiness should take over your soul, and you may feel like your heart is expanding. That is how you get the shift you so wish. Love is one of the basic human emotions, and one of the feelings that put you in the highest vibrating state. It can pull you out from the darkest of holes. Teach your soul about love, nourish it with love, and you will become supercharged with vibration.

3. *Be generous.* Generosity is another powerful feeling that can heighten your vibration. Greediness or stinginess is a low-vibrating feeling that makes you feel bad. It doesn't do anything for you. When you attach your happiness to something external, such as money, attention, or love, it gives the opposite effect of what you really want and desire. The key to feeling great about yourself is

generosity. When you feel how you want to live, it puts your body in a constant vibration state that can be helpful in the astral realm. Whatever you feel you really desire more of in life, give it out to somebody else. If you feel like you do not have any money, that is the best time to give to charity. If you feel lonely, it is the right time to help another person feel wanted by making them smile. If you feel like time is too short, invest some hours at a good cause. Doing things such as this teaches you that there is more to life than what you believe you don't have enough of.

4. *Forgive.* Blame is one of the emotions that radiate low-vibrational energy. Forgiveness is the direct opposite of blame. Working toward forgiveness at all times releases you of the lower energy from blame, and your vibrations go up the chart. Learn to forgive and forget as well if you can pull it off. When you forgive, the feeling of blame weighing on you will dissipate slowly, and your heart and body will feel lighter than usual. So, rather than blaming people, start forgiving them. Forgiveness is a way of both helping yourself and helping the people whom you forgive.

5. *Meditate regularly.* The truer you are, the higher your level of vibration. Meditation is a way of training yourself to live in the moment and be present. The more you practice meditation, especially mindfulness meditation, the higher your state of awareness becomes. The past is a figment of your mind, so is the future. However, the present is now, and it only tells the truth. Meditation greatly helps you increase your vibration level quickly to the point where you can fight immaterial astral beings if they so happen to confront you.

Incorporating these emotions into your life is bound to uplift every aspect of your life, not just your spiritual life. Therefore, make them a habit and do not just consider them a means to an end.

Chapter Eleven: Meeting Spirit Guides and Other Advanced Astral Travel Adventures

As you now know, the astral plane is also host to many benevolent spirits. Some of these spirits are there to help you when needed and serve as your teacher, to open up your mind to the true realities of the universe. Usually, each astral projector gets one particular spirit guide—one that is attached to your spirit. However, spirit guides are not typically just one being; you can have more than three spirit guides at a time. The one guide you see most often is your main spirit guide. Some guides are only there to help you for a brief moment in your life, whereas others will be with you until the end of time. Some guides only come to teach you one or two life lessons and help you with a quest, particularly spiritual ones. Several books have been written on how you can contact your spirit guides whenever you need them, but that is not the focus of this book. When you visit the astral dimension, you meet your spirit guides. But what happens when you meet them? Also, what are spirit guides really like? These are some of the questions people constantly ask about meeting spirit guides in the astral plane.

First, you should know that your spirit guide can be anybody, but they are not angels. Many people assume that spirit guides and angels are the same. The most basic thing you should know about spirit guides is that any being or entity can serve as your spirit guide. However, spirit guides are not automatically angels. The key difference between angels and spirit guides is that spirit guides are incarnated beings, while angels have never incarnated. Spirit guides are also classified into different categories, such as a healing guide, teacher guide, and master guide. Some people believe that angels have more important things to do than be someone's healing or teaching guide. People who think this are partly right, but the whole thing is not so black and white. Some people have reported having angels as their spirit guides, and that is okay.

The point is to help you understand the difference between the different types of guides in the astral plane and their role in your life.

It is not uncommon in the astral plane to meet your deceased loved ones serving as your spirit guide. If you meet a dead loved one in the astral plane, do not be surprised as they might have chosen to watch over you and protect you from the other side. For many people, this usually turns out to be their grandparent (s). Sometimes, your ancestors—people whom you have never met—may be your spirit guide. From generations ago, they have decided to serve as spirit guides for people from their bloodline. Even if you do not know them, don't be afraid to let them help you as they bear no malicious intent. Friends from your past lives may also serve as spirit guides. You may have chosen to incarnate, while close friends from your past chose to live that one life and enjoy the rest of their lives in the astral plane. As a result, they get the power to choose to help you from the other side. On the astral plane, time limitations or restrictions don't exist. Therefore, you may meet someone from your past life some 3,000 years ago. Maybe someone you even knew from the old Camelot. This happens to a lot of people.

Someone once reported meeting a friend from their past life in ancient Rome.

You may also meet general spirit helpers—people who have no past or present affiliation to you. You don't know them, but they choose to watch over you and help you navigate the universe in the right place. Sometimes, they may just appear to help you with a task you are working on because they have in-depth knowledge about that topic. Angels sometimes serve as spirit guides too. Obviously, they are not too busy to pass on helping people who may need their help. Ascended masters are also spirit guides. They are higher beings who have incarnated before. Ascended masters are those who have attained the peak of enlightenment. An example of an ascended master is the Buddha. Yes, you can meet the Buddha on the astral plane if he happens to be around. Other entities that you may meet in the higher astral realm are elementals, deities, extra-terrestrial, and spirit animals.

Factors That Determine Who Your Spirit Guide Is

It is hard to say whom you will get as your spirit guide as several factors determine it. For example, an expert in esoteric healing abilities and spiritual tasks is highly unlikely to get a family member as their spirit guide. This is because they already have extensive knowledge and may require someone with higher knowledge to be their guide. The four factors that are used to determine whom you get as your guide include:

- Energetic fingerprint
- Level of knowledge
- Relationship ties
- Pre-incarnation contract

Energetic Fingerprint

An energetic fingerprint contains everything you want to know about yourself as an energy being. It is the blueprint of your being, which has everything about your energetic makeup. Information regarding your soul archetype, chakras, auric colors, and elements are all in the energetic fingerprint. Each person has an energetic fingerprint that is unique to them. In the astral world, spirits recognize you by your energetic fingerprint. Not all beings in the higher realms have names. Some don't even know what names are. So, you need to find a way to identify yourself with them. When you get a guide that isn't from your past life or the current one, it is because your energy reading aligns with that guide's energy reading. In the astral world, similar beings attract. You may have comparable elements with the spirit guide that you get, or it could just be that your auric colors match each other.

Level of Knowledge

You get guides that match your level of knowledge about the astral planes and the universe. If you are still a beginner to astral travel, you cannot expect to get an advanced guide with infinite wisdom to share about the universe. The guide (s) you get is one that can teach you something at the level of your spiritual knowledge to facilitate growth. Vibration may also be a factor in this regard. You also get guides that are in tandem with your vibration level. If you are an amateur astral traveler, you can't get a professor as your spirit guide. You get someone suitable for the level you are at.

Relationship Ties

Obviously, this means getting people you have a tie or bond with. You don't necessarily have to share blood ties; it could just be someone you used to be emotionally connected to. Your dead loved ones, past lives, friends, and ancestors are all people you meet because of the relationship tie you have with them.

Pre-Incarnation Contract

This is quite straightforward. When you incarnate, you don't get your whole soul group. Some decide to stay behind in the spiritual realms to help others. So, some of the people you come across as spirit guides are sometimes people who have a pre-incarnation contract to watch over you while you are on Earth. It is a sort of agreement that they have made with your soul, and they have no choice but to fulfill that agreement.

Apart from meeting your spirit guides, there are other adventures that you may have on the astral realm. One of these is gaining access to the Akashic Records.

Accessing the Akashic Records

The akashic record contains information about everything that has ever and will ever be. Every individual has their own book in the akashic record: a sum of their complete human experience. The akashic records are described as a never-ending library. You cannot access the akashic record from the prime material plane or the physical realm, but it is believed that you can when you are in your astral form. The akasha is on the etheric plane. Visiting the akashic records to find out information about your past—and possibly your future—is one of the adventures that you can have when you are in your astral form. Historically, it is said that only people who have been deemed worthy are allowed access to the akashic records. Therefore, it is not something you can do in your first few visits to the astral realm.

Accessing the akashic records when you are in astral form is possible because the astral plane is a place of will, where you use your mind to ask for the things you desire. If you so wish, you can will yourself from the astral plane to the akashic records. Before you try to do this, you should have set your intention for astral travel. Keep in mind that you always need to have a purpose when you astral project, so make "reaching the hall of records" your goal whenever you plan to astral travel to reach the akashic records. It should be set as one specific goal in your mind, and there should be nothing else. Now that you know this, how do you access the akashic records?

As usual, you need to use the astral projection technique that works for you to project yourself into your astral form. Once this form is separated from your physical body, you can then will yourself to appear in the hall of records by simply thinking, "I wish to go to the Akashic records/the hall of record." You don't have to say it exactly like that, but it should be something along that line. Once you will it, you will find yourself in the hall as if you were dreaming. Knowing that the main form of communication in the astral form is the mind, whatever you need to find in the hall of records must be willed with your mind.

Tips for Accessing the Akashic Record

• *State your intention for coming to the Akashic records in your mind.* Of course, you should have put some thought into this before even coming to the hall. Don't attempt to access the hall until you have a definite reason why you want to do that. What do you want to know? How might knowing this thing help you? Not knowing the exact thing you are looking for in the akashic record may lead to a disorganized search—which means you may not find any helpful information. An example of a possible reason for searching the akashic record might be to find out where your current relationship with your partner is headed.

• *Before you take your astral form, you can write down specific questions to seek answers to in the akashic records.* Make a list of the things you want to know and the questions you want to ask. Make them as specific as possible. For example, you may ask, "What was my purpose in my last life? Is it correlated to my current profession in my present life?" You can also ask things regarding where you used to live or what jobs you used to have.

- *Don't ask vague or irrelevant questions when you are in the hall of records.* Ask questions that help you proffer solutions to any problems you may be facing in your present life. Ask questions that can guide you in making decisions that could affect your entire life. If you have been facing a particular problem and there is no solution in sight, ask about the best solution. For instance, you may ask, "I am currently thinking about changing my job to settle for my passion, but I don't know if that is going to be a good decision or not."

- *Do not ask more than one question at a time.* Remember that your mind is your communication tool in the hall of records. So, don't actually speak out; just think about whatever question you have. Asking one question at a time makes it easier to get clearer answers. Focus on each topic you are interested in at a time. For instance, ask questions about your relationship before moving on to questions about your career, health, or any other topic you might be interested in.

- *While in the akashic records, keep yourself relaxed, so you don't get pulled out of your astral form before you get the answers to your questions.* Occasionally, breathe deeply as you remain in the hall. Stay calm, and keep your emotions in check. Don't be too excited or anxious about getting the answers you seek.

Once you have accessed the akashic records, how do you find the information you need?

- *Think out loud and ask to be granted access to your book in the hall of records.* If you wish, you can ask out loud by saying something along the line of "I seek past information about myself. May I please access my book to find the information that I seek?" After you ask this question, breathe in deeply and clear your mind. Do not be surprised if you don't get a reply immediately. You may need to ask more than once before you are granted access to your records.

- *Wait.* You can't do anything else except wait for the information you seek to be granted. Contrary to what you see in the movies, higher beings don't always come out from behind the shelves and hand your book to you! Instead, the information will appear in your consciousness. Continue to breathe deeply while you wait for the thing you seek. Note that the information may come in different ways via your five senses. You may see, taste, smell, feel, or hear something. That is the akashic hall's way of conveying the message. For example, if you ask where your present relationship will lead, you might see the shape of a ring in your mind's eye, which likely means that it will result in marriage. Alternatively, you might taste something sweet like cake, which could mean the same thing.

- *In some cases, you may immediately sense the presence of a higher being.* You may even see this being depending on the level of your clairvoyant abilities. If you sense anyone near you, reintroduce yourself out loud and ask your question once again. The higher being might be the keeper of your records or someone just there to do some other task. Regardless, ask your question, and they might help you.

- *After you succeed in accessing your records, you can then will yourself back home.* Once you are back in your physical form, you will need to interpret the information you get. Take a pen and paper and use it to decipher what you were given. Sometimes, you will need to visit the akashic records several times before finally getting the full answer to one question.

You can always repeat the steps above to continue learning about your past in the hall of records. You can make your visits weekly or bi-weekly. Remember to keep it one topic at a time when you access the akashic records.

Sex on the Astral Plane?

Astral sex is becoming something of a trend, with more people reporting it. You are likely already familiar with the feelings and sensations of physical sex. Still, you probably did not know that you can also participate in sexual intercourse while you are out of your body—and the people who have stated that it is even better than physical sex. You cannot know that unless you try it, though. So, if you are up to it, there is a whole part of the astral realm dedicated to those who want to revel in sexual pleasure without having to do it the usual way.

Astral sex is also referred to as non-corporeal sex, and there are multiple ways you can engage in it. You can decide to make it dream sex, which involves having sex with a dream character of your choice. You can take your astral form and have sex with another person while they are still in their physical form. Or, you can get your partner to go to the astral plane with you and unleash unbridled passion. It all depends on the choice you make.

Dream Sex

It is safe and absolutely normal to have sex in your dream. Plus, just because it is a dream doesn't mean it will be devoid of pleasure. It's just you and the dream character you develop in your subconscious mind. This is possible when you induce a lucid dreaming state. As pleasurable as it is, you don't have to do it if it isn't something that you really want.

Astral-Corporeal Sex

This is where one person is in their physical form, and the other person is out of the body. If you have both already agreed to it, all you need to do is enter your astral form and then channel your astral form to wherever the other person's physical body is while they sleep. Then, you simply charge your energy onto theirs since you can see their astral form and will sexual thoughts into their energy field. This will lead to you experiencing a sexual bliss similar to an orgasm, but not from any body part. Your sexual partner will have a wet dream involving you or become sexually aroused while still unconscious. If your partner is great at lucid dreaming, this experience may trigger a lucid dream. Otherwise, they will wake up the next day and remember dreaming about you.

Astral-Astral

If your partner is also an astral projector, this is something you can achieve together. Both of you just need to induce your astral states, travel deep into the astral plane, and engage in sexual intercourse consciously. However, you may find this a little bit tricky as the astral realm isn't always predictable. If you can, pick a spot and time ahead of the chosen day. Also, ensure you are at the same astral frequency. The closer you both are emotionally, the higher your chances of pulling non-corporeal sex off.

Other than this, some people have reported having sex with entities they meet on the astral plane. This is not safe, and you should never attempt it as some of these entities may just be there to drain you of your energy.

Chapter Twelve: How to Return to Physical Body

The idea that the soul can become permanently separated from your body during astral projection is one that has pervaded mainstream media for too long. You see it in the movies, where an antagonist's soul is separated from their physical body and then sent deep into the lower astral plane, never to return. Unless you die, your soul cannot separate completely from your body. Coming back to your physical form after an out-of-body experience is quite a straightforward process. However, some believe that it is possible to go to the astral plane without being able to return to your physical body. In fact, there is a popular myth about people dying in the astral realm. People who say such things have never had an out-of-body experience or bothered to find out more about it. As a result, many fear to engage in astral projection practice. Most of the information you find online regarding these misconceptions stem from what people watch in films or read in fairytale books. Similarly, some people believe that staying too long in the astral plane can also leave your body vulnerable to negative entities that will take possession of it, so you can never go back. Again, these are blatant untruths.

Going back to your physical body after astral travel is not difficult as long as you know how to go about it. In some instances, your soul may even return to your body by itself if it feels like you are in some form of danger and cannot handle it. To return to your physical body, you need to know what the silver cord is. The silver cord links your soul to your physical body and guides you into your astral form and back when you are done. Thanks to the silver cord, your soul will always remain connected to the physical body even when you are in your astral form. The silver cord is strong and durable; it isn't something that can just snap or be cut. Plus, it can stretch beyond limits. Even if you tried, you could not cut the silver cord. Therefore, no one can completely cut you off from your physical body.

The silver cord has a very smooth texture that can never get tangled or form knots. It cannot be removed, but it can stretch from place to place. When you enter your astral form and fly upwards to the higher planes, the silver cord follows you without detaching from your body. This cord is not made from a material item; it is pure energy—which is why it can't be severed or eliminated. So, you can be sure that there is no way anyone can sever the connection between your physical and astral body. Neither can this connection become weak. The link between your soul and body remains intact even in the astral form.

Now to return to your physical body: As you have read, the process is simple. You just follow your silver cord back to your body. When you enter an astral state, your silver cord marks the way you travel. Once you are done exploring the astral plane, you can return to your body by tracing the cord back. In your astral form, time and matter are non-existent. Distance also does not exist. If you choose, you can fly at the speed of a jet. Or, you can run with the speed of light. Returning to your body may not even take a second; it is more about your mind than your body. Keeping in mind that the astral world is a place of will, you only need to will yourself to return to your body.

Understandably, you may experience some difficulty getting back to your body, but it is usually nothing to worry about. If you struggle, just go back to the astral realm, explore some more, and then try again. When you are astral traveling, and something threatening happens, the soul will instantly return to your physical body. The best thing you can do is to prepare some form of protection for your energy field.

Chapter Thirteen: After-Effects and Integration

Once your soul has reconnected with your body, you will jar awake immediately. At this moment, you have a heightened sense of awareness that can be put to good use for further enlightenment. The best thing to do after returning to the physical realm and your physical body is to meditate and get your mind back in tune with reality. Just as meditation is great for calming your mind before you begin your astral travel, it is also very effective for returning your mind and body to its normal state. There are no negative after-effects of returning from the astral realm. The effects are usually positive. In just one astral experience, your mind can become incredibly enlightened. You will certainly notice a major change in your outlook on the world and issues relating to yourself and the people around you. Meditation can make this even more enhanced. Mindfulness meditation opens your mind and increases your capacity to remain aware and alert of the present moment. Therefore, when you practice mindfulness right after astral projection, it helps you remain grounded after what you have just experienced. This means that you can keep the sensations of being in the astral world for as long as you want, probably until your next visit to the astral realm.

Meditating right after integrating back into your body is also a way to ensure that you get the best out of your astral experience. For example, if you access the akashic record via your astral form, meditating right after you return to your physical form can help you open your mind, so you can decipher the messages conveyed to you in the hall of records. Meditation, particularly mindfulness meditation, increases your sense of clarity and calmness about the amazing experience you have just had.

Out-of-Body Meditation

Out-of-body meditation can be practiced after returning from the astral plane and right before integrating into your body. Meditating right after an out-of-body experience helps enhance the after-effects of your visit to the higher planes. To meditate while still out of the body:

- Sit your astral form in the air right above your physical body. Your mind might be in a state of excitement due to the realm you are coming from. Calm it down and let your body relax.

- Remain in that position for as long as you wish. Be still. Your subconscious mind will absorb your experience in the astral realm better this way.

- Focus and let the mind enlighten itself from its journey on the astral plane.

- After a while, return to your physical body.

Do not meditate for too long as you want to avoid falling asleep while still in your astral form.

Journaling

Apart from meditation, another thing you should do after each out-of-body experience is to journal your experience. It has been proven that documenting and measuring each attempt you make can make progress far easier and faster. It is the same with astral projection, astral travel, and out-of-body experiences. To journal your OBE attempts, use a page-per-view journal. You do not always have to write something in-depth—just put down how you feel right after your experience. Don't wait until you forget how the experience made you feel. Keeping a journal is an incredible way of monitoring your astral projection efforts and finding where to improve. If you keep a journal for your astral travels, it provides insight into what is really effective for you, serves as a reminder for your successes and failures, and, most importantly, helps you stay motivated to become an experienced astral projector and traveler in no time.

- *Establish a practice routine*

Without a routine, you may find it difficult to accomplish anything concerning astral travel. It takes much discipline to keep up with astral projection, especially when you haven't had many successful attempts. Get a good journal where you can write something down in ink—do not keep the journal on your phone. Writing your experience down with a pen and paper makes you appreciate the wholesomeness of your astral travels. However, if you want, you can use your phone or computer to keep notes of everything in the astral realm. After one month of journaling, you should have successfully established a routine and made astral projection practice a habit.

- *Evaluate progress, monitor success, and examine failures*

Some people have good results when they first try astral projection. Merely getting close to having an actual OBE is a success. However, they end up giving up when they try many times without getting the experience they crave. Usually, this happens due to forgetfulness—they forget the extent to which they succeeded and what was left to make it a complete success. Recording your experiences can help you avoid this. When you record your progress, success, and failures in OBE practice, you are more likely to improve. Why? Because you are monitoring your progress. You know what you are doing right and what you appear not to be doing right. So, keep a journal and actively look for ways to improve to find the technique that suits you the most. Only then will you achieve more tangible results.

- *Improve the realness*

Astral projection is one thing that may feel intangible, but writing it down makes the experiences feel more *real*. Even if you miss a few times, the misses will still feel real to you when you write them down. If you have ever kept a dream journal, you will know what this feels like. When you write down dreams immediately after waking up, they tend to stay with you in your subconscious. But the ones you don't record will disappear quickly. So, start writing your experiences down, and they will feel more real to you. More importantly, your achievements will become more apparent, and that will motivate you to keep the practice going.

Finally, make sure you set up a schedule for your OBE practice. Choose a day of the week to practice and make sure you do not ever miss it. As you improve, you can increase the number of times you practice every week. Regular practice is usually the key to unlocking your full astral projection capabilities. So, continue to practice and explore the astral realm to gain a deeper sense of enlightenment and awareness. After a while, you may even unlock your psychic abilities.

Chapter Fourteen: Energy Healing

If you plan to become a regular astral projector, you must know how to facilitate energy healing when needed. You do not have to master reiki healing before you can heal yourself. In Chapter One, you learned that the auric field can misbehave when the energy centers are out of sync. This can affect your ability to take your astral form. Whenever you feel like your energy centers are misaligned, masters of healing have proven four essential techniques to help heal and restore your energy levels—precisely as an energy healer would help you restore your powers.

- **Connect to the cosmic energy flow**

Whenever your energy points feel out of sync, you can connect to the universal point of energy to tap into the never-ending energy source and heal yourself. Once you do this, you will experience an abundance of energy and increase your vibrations to become more powerful. The easiest way to tap into the cosmic energy flow is to visualize a grounding cord extending from your seat to the ground to connect with the energy center of the Earth. As you feel this connection, breathe it in and allow the energy to come through the same cord that connects you to the Earth's energy center. Feel the rush of energy flow up your body, from your feet to your legs, stomach, chest, neck, heart, and head. Allow the energy to wash over your head as though you are under a waterfall. Then, visualize the rain of energy, making its way back into the ground to its center once again. This visualization exercise can easily connect and recharge your body with energy from the universal flow center.

- **Regularly cleanse your aura**

When your energy field is contaminated, drained, or out of balance, it affects your aura. External energy can make your aura foggy due to a lack of proper energy flow. Add that to dull auric colors, and you will be vulnerable the next time you attempt going to the astral plane. Hence, it is essential to cleanse your auric field regularly, so it keeps a vibrant appearance. Dull colors in the aura can produce a low and static vibration that makes it impossible to operate in the astral plane with a clear mind. To cleanse your auric field and restore its colors, sit somewhere quiet and join your left hand's fingers to form a cone. Then, put the coned fingers on the right side of your head, a little above the forehead. Repeat the same thing with the right hand, but put them on the left side of your hairline. Remain in this position for about fifteen seconds and then swap the hands. Wait for another fifteen seconds. Each chakra—your energy points—can be likened to a Christmas light. Using this technique means that you are plugging in each center with the next to light up your entire auric field.

- **Build a shield around your energy field**

When you talk with others or do something as simple as exchange greetings, you are unknowingly engaging in energy exchange. You may have observed that some people seem to contaminate your mood, while others light it up. This is because every person you spend time around has their own way of affecting your energy field. They may not know that they are doing this. Sometimes, you unsuspectingly get into an unfavorable energy exchange with the wrong people. This then affects your auric field and everything else tied to it, including your mind, astral spirit, and physical body. So, shielding yourself from negativity is essential. Keeping a shield around your energy field whenever you exchange with people will prevent your energy field from being saturated or oversaturated by negative energy. This helps preserve your energy to keep energy vampires away.

To build a shield around your auric field, sit in a quiet space, and visualize a very bright light of any color. Let the light sparkle from your upper abdomen to every part of your body, so it saturates your auric field. It is akin to putting a thick and soft blanket over your body to keep your warm and centered. This technique will keep you protected from potential energy vampires.

Chapter Fifteen: Increasing your Clairvoyant Abilities Via Astral Projection

Clairvoyance is a primary psychic ability that literally means "clear seeing." This points to an ability to see within and beyond all things. Clairvoyance allows you to look within the knowledge in your soul and other souls existing within the universe, including those from the past and ones yet to manifest. Experts believe that everyone has clairvoyant abilities, even though the degree varies from person to person. The good thing is that astral projection and astral travel can be very effective in improving your clairvoyant abilities. When you visit the astral plane, there are some steps you can take to expand your abilities. Just as exercise can help build your physical muscles, astral projection exercises can help build your psychic muscles.

Astral projection practice is a time to release your fears, including your clairvoyant fears. One way or another, you might have experienced your clairvoyance oddly manifesting itself. Unsuspecting, you may have blocked it to your subconscious due to not recognizing it for what it is. So, the first thing you need to do is release your fears regarding your gift while in the astral plane. While meditating to project into the astral plane, you can simply affirm to yourself that, "I will let go of my fears regarding my psychic abilities in the astral plane." Affirming it to yourself before you leave makes it much easier to do. Once you get to the astral plane or simply enter your astral form, how do you make this possible?

- *Find a quiet place on the astral plane.* Make sure you do this in the higher astral plane to avoid getting attacked by a lower astral entity while you are engrossed in the task. If you aren't on the higher plane, create an armor of light around yourself to keep negative entities away.

- *Next, try to locate the source of your fear.* Doing this in the astral form would be much more comfortable than on the physical plane since your consciousness is the only active and aware thing in the astral realm. Hence, it should be easier to navigate and search through. Identify the source of the fear.

- *Once you know the source, use positive affirmation to will away the fear.* Say something like, "I let go of the fear blocking me from accessing my full clairvoyant abilities."

- *Repeat this affirmation as many times as you want.*

Do this three times in a row every time you are in the astral plane, and you will lose your fear of clairvoyance in no time.

Once you get rid of your fears, the next step is to tune in with your third eye chakra. The chakra is one of your energy points and is the reason why you have clairvoyant abilities. Since the third eye chakra is an energy point and the astral body is one of the layers of energy, tuning in with your third eye is usually easier on the astral plane.

In your astral form:

- Close your eyes and focus on the spot between both of your eyebrows. Envision it as a horizontal oval shape in between your eyes.

- Try noticing if the eyelid of this third eye is close or opened. If it is closed, gently ask it to open and repeat the request until you feel the eye open.

- When the third eye opens, you will feel an instant rush of warmth in your body. This happens because you are embracing a part of you that had been previously blocked.

- If you do not get it right the first time, keep practicing until you do.

Remember that you can also do this exercise in your physical form. However, it may not be as effective because you are closer to the energy points when you are in your astral form.

After literally opening your third eye, you may start seeing floating objects, shadows, lights, and pictures. These will usually come in different forms: full-color, black, white, gray, lifelike, or cartoonish. At first, you likely will not understand the images. To make them more evident to you, practice visualization before you start using your power to ask and answer specific questions. Visually recreate the images in your mind and make them more prominent and brighter to clearly see and interpret them. This will require much of your willpower and intention, primarily when you practice in your astral form. The astral plane is an energy point, which means it naturally requires more energy to exist on the plane. If you regularly practice the energy healing methods discussed in the previous chapter, you will never have to worry about your energy source being depleted on the astral plane.

Start using your clairvoyant abilities to answer questions. Make sure you keep the questions as specific as possible. Do not ask open-ended questions like, "What is my future like?" Instead, make it specific like, "Will I still have this ability in the next fifteen years?" The questions you ask should be formulated so that the answers you get can be decoded more easily. Leave general questions alone until you become more advanced in your skills. Once you begin receiving mental images, start trying to interpret them so that you can know whatever it is they are telling you. If some of the images do not mean anything to you, use your time in the astral plane to consult with your spirit guides and other higher entities to clarify the meanings of the images and symbols. Answers from your spirit guide may come through feelings, taste, thoughts, or sounds—just as it is in the akashic hall of records. Don't despair if the answer you get seems vague or random; it is normal. All you need to do is repeat your questions to the higher beings so they can keep answering in different ways until you finally understand.

In the meantime, keep a journal of your clairvoyant experiences. You should not write down these experiences in the same journal you use for your OBE journey—get another journal. Keeping a journal, as you already know, helps you monitor your progress. In this case, it will provide more insight into other psychic abilities that you may possess. If possible, find someone that also has psychic abilities and is into astral projection. You can help each other to develop your skills and become more powerful.

Do not forget to meditate and practice visualization regularly as both actions can further enhance your clairvoyant skills. Furthermore, make sure to share your experiences with your spirit guide and any other higher being on the astral plane.

Conclusion

Congratulations, you are on your way to becoming an accomplished astral projector. There are two sides to learning astral projection: 1) Having the right resources to get all the information you need, and 2) Putting that information into practice.

This book has covered pretty much everything about astral projection. You have learned about the basic and advanced astral projection techniques and the right way to put them into practice. More importantly, you have learned how to remain protected in the astral realm. Therefore, all that's left is to practice and get started on your journey to spiritual enlightenment and awareness.

Enjoy your journey!

Part 2: Lucid Dreaming for Beginners

What You Need to Know About Controlling Your Dreams to Improve Your Sleep and Creativity

Introduction

We all dream, and our dreams can be happy, exhilarating, exciting, frightening, or intriguing. Our unique ability to dream has been a fascinating aspect that science has been trying to explore since the dawn of civilization. Dreams are like live-action movies, which signify a lot of things. In your dreams, the sky is the limit, and there isn't anything you cannot try or do. You can be a magician, explore your wildest ideas, and delve into your subconscious.

Do you always remember your dreams? Chances are, you often forget about them the moment you open your eyes.

With lucid dreaming, you can recollect your dreams and even control them. Lucid dreaming is a fascinating concept which teaches you to become consciously aware of yourself while in dreamland. It makes you the writer, director, actor, and producer of your own play. If you ever thought about exploring some of your ideas but lack the confidence to do it, lucid dreaming will come in handy. Lucid dreaming is the key to discovering your inner self – the world within you – and your subconscious. From exploring your goals and fantasies to living your dreams, you can do it all.

In this book, you will learn about dreams and their meaning, about lucid dreaming, and the different benefits it offers. You will also learn about the relationship between astral projection, shamanic journeying, and lucid dreaming, some tips to prepare for learning more about lucid dreaming, and steps to prepare for an enhanced lucid dreaming experience.

Apart from that, you will discover various lucid dreaming techniques ideal for beginners and some advanced techniques, too. In this book, you will find practical and simple tips for exploring the lucid dreamscape, meeting spirit guides, and how to protect yourself during lucid dreams. Some helpful tips about avoiding certain mistakes when you are lucid dreaming are included in this book.

So, are you ready to learn more about all this? Are you excited to start your personal journey into the world of lucid dreams? If yes, let's get started without further ado!

Chapter One: What Are Dreams?

Dreams are a mystery to us, and scientists and psychologists have long been studying them to try to understand more. They might seem weird, strange, or even terrifying, but your dreams have a meaning. It is believed that your dreams help to maintain your physical and psychological health. There are many theories on dreams that have stated that dreams do have a purpose, but some theories state that dreams may have no purpose at all. Once you learn about lucid dreaming, your perception of dreams will change.

Psychologists have conducted thorough research on dreams. Their research dates back to the early 1900s, and they have performed psychological analyses of people's dreams for many years. The psychologists analyzed the dreams of their patients in dream laboratories and used the information they obtained to develop their theories. Sigmund Freud held out the first theory of dreams; he claimed that dreams only helped the person having them sleep well through the night. Freud also believed that people only had dreams when they were hungry, had a sexual urge, or needed to use the washroom. His theory was later contradicted when someone claimed that a person dreams at least five times when he is in the REM (Rapid Eye Movement) stage of his sleep cycle.

Carl Jung stated the next famous theory. He was an ardent follower of Freud, but he believed there was a different purpose behind dreams, and broke away from the Freudian theory to state a new theory. He claimed that a person had dreams to compensate for the parts of his total personality or psyche that were underdeveloped when he was awake.

Calvin Hall contradicted this theory with his own. To confirm his theory, he asked his students to maintain a dream journal for two weeks. He believed that a person would always represent himself in his dream. This meant that a person who is an introvert when he is awake is also an introvert in his dreams.

Other dream theorists believe dreams are the solutions to all our problems. They believe dreams only occur when a person is facing an unsolvable problem in life. Many psychologists tried to obtain evidence to back this theory, and it was during this research that they were finally able to establish the use of dreams based these on different cultural beliefs.

Why Do We Dream?

Freud had claimed that every person was a poet, intentionally or not, and that dreams were much like poetry. Poets use muses or experiences in their lives to write, and they express their emotions through poems. In the same way, you create images and situations in your dreams, and when you combine them with various events in your life, you elicit an emotional response within yourself. Dreams are stories that run through your unconscious or subconscious mind, and Freud believed these were not based on logic. Dreams are like motion pictures starring our emotions, fears, desires, and everything else buried in the subconscious.

Let us assume you argued with your friend this morning, and you were unable to get your point across. When you have a dream later tonight, you may find yourself in the same situation but arguing differently, and perhaps making your point quite well. Dreams help you change the outcome of situations that have already occurred. Events in your dream are based on the thoughts and emotions in your subconscious.

Another example can be one where you are taking an exam. Before the exam season starts, you may have many dreams where you either ace or fail the examination. You may have such a dream either because you want to be the valedictorian or because you fear examinations. When you are wide-awake, you cannot study for the test because you are worried about how you will fare. This still does not help us understand why we dream, but there are five theories regarding that.

Theory One: Practice Responses

Did you ever dream about falling off a cliff, fighting an enemy, or being chased by a dog? Well, you are not the first person to have such a dream. You tend to have such dreams during your REM sleep because your amygdala, the part of your brain that stimulates your fight-or-flight response, works at its peak. Antti Revonsuo, a Finnish cognitive scientist, stated that people dream only during their REM sleep.

It is during your REM sleep that your brain works as if it perceives danger because the amygdala is functioning at its peak. The part of your brain that controls your motor ability also works at its peak, and you may not be moving your limbs when you are asleep, but you can still have a dream where you are taking a stroll down the beach or fighting for your life. Antti proved that dreams are your stage, and that is where your brain rehearses a potential threat. You rehearse your reactions – both physical and emotional – during your dreams. It is for this reason some people kick in their sleep or wake up crying.

Theory Two: Sifting Through Memories

Your brain limits the number of images it stores in your conscious memory. If you remembered every image from every event that happened in life, your brain would be clogged with irrelevant information. Your brain sorts through your memories in your subconscious mind and tries to identify those memories it should store and those it should get rid of. If you want to understand this better, think about how the mind works in the movie *Inside Out*. In that movie, a group of people "lived" inside the brain, looking at their subconscious memories and tossing them out when they turned grey. This is exactly how your mind works. There is no team, but your brain does flush out any unwanted memories and images.

Similarly, your brain segregates the memories through your dreams. Matt Wilson, a professor at MIT's Center for Learning and Memory, strongly backs this theory. In his experiments on rats, he put them in a maze throughout the day and monitored their neuron patterns. Wilson paid close attention to their neuron patterns during their REM sleep and discovered that the patterns were the same as those when the rats were running in the maze. He claimed that the brain uses dreams to identify the worthiness of a memory. Your sleep turns all the information you have into strong memories, helping you make decisions in the future.

Theory Three: Dreaming is Defragmentation

When you buy a new laptop or desktop, the first thing you do is separate your drives. You create the number of drives you want in the space provided by the device. In the same way, your brain also tries to identify the importance of all your memories. Francis Crick and Graeme Mitchison claimed that a person dreamed in order to forget. They meant that your brain tries to identify whether the data it contains, in the form of memories, is useful or not. It tries to establish a connection between your memories, attempting to identify those it should keep in the active memory, and those it should move to your subconscious memory. Your brain uses this method to go through your memories to identify those connections that are important and those that are not.

Theory Four: Your Personal Psychotherapist

Ernest Hartmann, a doctor at Tufts, proposed that dreams help us confront those emotions we refuse to acknowledge. He focused on what people learn when they dream. He stated the theory that your brain uses images and a sequence of events to help you face those emotions your conscious mind is scared to look at. When you dream, you deal with all your difficult emotions in a safe place, which is similar to psychotherapy. You can consider dreams to be your therapists, and your bed is the therapeutic couch. You observe all your emotions and thoughts, and let your brain tell you what you should do to prevent an emotional imbalance. Through your dreams, you learn to accept certain truths that you would have never been able to accept consciously.

Theory Five: No Meaning At All

We mentioned earlier that some people now believe there is no meaning to your dreams. Modern theorists have argued that the brain fires images at random, and some of these situations may not have anything to do with something that occurred when you were conscious. Your dreams are like a film where you are the hero, and the story is not dependent on your life.

Some Facts

Did you ever experience any terrifying, weird, fascinating, exciting, and fun dreams? Well, we have all experienced a variety of dreams, but might not remember most of them. Before we learn to look at how you can remember them, let us look at some interesting facts about dreams.

Everyone Dreams

Yes, everyone, including men, women, babies, and even animals, dream. People who claim to have a dreamless sleep are mistaken. They dream, too, but do not remember them when they wake up. Psychologists believe there is enough evidence to prove that everyone dreams, and a person may have more than ten dreams each night. They also found that each dream lasts only for ten minutes, but you may have some dreams that last for more than forty-five minutes. Over a lifetime the average person will dream for a total of more than six years.

You Cannot Remember All of Your Dreams

Have you ever had this wonderful dream and wanted to remember it in the morning? You may have even told yourself to remember it during the dream or a half-awake moment immediately thereafter, but you wake up in the morning with only a feeling that you have forgotten something wonderful. Allan Hobson, a dream researcher, stated that you forget close to 95 percent of your dreams a few minutes after you wake up. He scanned the brains of his subjects while they slept, and found that the frontal lobe of the brain, essential in storing memory, was inactive when they were dreaming.

You May Have Colors in Your Dreams

Many psychologists believe that at least eighty percent of your dreams have a lot of colors. Some people claim they only dream in black and white. But if you were to wake someone up during their REM sleep and ask them to choose a color that they just saw in their dream, they would pick any color other than black or white.

You Can Control Your Dreams

That does sound fascinating, does it not? People can use various lucid dreaming techniques to control their dreams. When you master this technique, you will be aware of the fact that you are dreaming, although you are asleep. Psychologists believe that at least five out of ten people have had lucid dreams, but they are not aware of it. There are quite a few individuals who have frequent lucid dreams. The concept of lucid dreaming is covered in detail later in the book.

Dreams Can Paralyze You

During your REM sleep, the part of your brain that deals with motor functions is latent. You may have had a dream where you were being chased by a dog and woken up terrified. You may have wanted to move your muscles to snap out of the dream, but you found it hard or even impossible. This is called sleep paralysis, and it is not permanent. You may feel paralyzed even after you wake up, but this feeling only lasts no more than ten minutes. There may have been dreams in which you were flailing your arms around and screaming, or felt your breath catching in your throat. During dream paralysis, none of those actions actually happen.

Dream Interpretation

Carl Jung is one of the founding fathers of dream interpretation, and he believed that dreams were like a window into your unconscious mind. Jung claimed that when a person was dreaming, he was identifying different solutions to problems that he had faced or might face when he was conscious.

Jung was an ardent follower of Freud, but he disagreed with his theories and began to research dream interpretation. He said that only the dreamer could interpret their dreams. He said that certain common symbols could be interpreted, but only the dreamer could interpret the other symbols that are unique to him. There are dream dictionaries describing the meaning of the objects frequently found in dreams. The next section of this chapter helps you identify how you can interpret your dreams!

Do your dreams have a hidden meaning?

When you have had a dream, first ask yourself whether that dream is of any significance to you. If it is, you will have to ask yourself if the dream has any meaning to it.

Have you ever had a dream in which you were falling off a cliff? You might have been rolling off the bed at the very same time. Your subconscious mind is conveying a message to you in the form of a dream, telling you that you are rolling off your bed. Dreams that are related to the physical environment you are in have little or no hidden meaning. For instance, if you were to have a dream where a loud noise was being made, it may not have any drastic impact on your life because it is just a reflection of the fact that a noisy truck is passing by, or there is thunder in the distance. Your subconscious mind often incorporates the happenings in your immediate physical environment into your dreams. For instance, you might hear the doorbell ringing in your dream. In reality, the baby monitor might have been buzzing. Your subconscious is sending you a message asking you to wake up because of the noise.

Have you ever had a nightmare after watching a horror movie? The emotions and fear that you had experienced while watching the movie can be translated into your dreams. This is why external circumstances that bring about a certain emotional response from you have a strong and deep impact on your dreams.

Certain elements are often found in the dreams of most people. These dreams elicit a wide range of emotions, and can be interpreted easily.

Common Dreams and their Interpretation

The most common dreams every individual has had on numerous occasions are discussed here. Irrespective of whether it's getting lost or falling, each dream conveys a specific meaning.

Falling Dreams

Falling dreams are very common dreams. They are memorable dreams. These dreams indicate that you are afraid of losing or letting go. They also indicate that you are anxious about failing after success.

Nude Dreams

There are times when you might have had dreams where you found it difficult to cover yourself fully. If you have had this dream, it shows that you are afraid of letting yourself close to anyone. You are vulnerable when exposed to others.

Floating Dreams

In these dreams, you find yourself becoming weightless and flying throughout the world your dream has created. Such dreams symbolize a deep desire for freedom.

Danger

These dreams commonly have a danger that might be approaching you. You are usually rendered helpless since you are unable to move. Such dreams might be indicators that there is a danger that might come in your way. They help you identify a solution via your dream.

Chasing Dreams

Dreams in which a known or unknown pursuer is chasing you indicate that you are feeling threatened in life.

Exam Dreams

This dream is often considered to be a mirrored dream. In these dreams, you are usually dreaming about being tested. These dreams signify self-evaluation. The questions in the examination are commonly related to various aspects of your personality.

Common dreams are a fascinating subject for researchers. They have found that every human being, even from different cultures, has experienced a variety of these dreams. Some psychologists have a theory that states human beings have these common dreams due to the interactions that they have with other people regularly.

How to Analyze Your Dreams

The biggest myth about the analysis of dreams is that there are rules that need to be followed word for word. This is, however, false, since every person is different. Jeffrey Sumber, a clinical psychotherapist, said that a dream could only be understood when an individual understood himself better. There are, however, certain guidelines that you can follow to make it easier for you to understand and analyze your dreams.

Maintain a Record of Your Dreams

The first step toward analyzing your dreams is to make a note of them. Sumber also said that when you note down your dreams, you are drawing the content out of your unconscious. If you feel that you cannot remember a dream, keep a journal by your bed and make a note saying, 'No dreams to record.' You will notice that within a span of two weeks, you start remembering your dreams!

Identify Your Emotions in the Dream

Ask yourself questions. Identify whether you were scared or remorseful or happy in the dream. Are those feelings dormant or active when you wake up in the morning? The final question should be whether or not you were comfortable with those feelings.

Identify the Elements of Your Dream

You might feature in your dreams in multiple ways. You will find a clear distinction between yourself and your characters in the dream. You will have to understand your emotions toward your characters in your dreams, too. They may be recurring elements in your dreams. Make a note of those and pay close attention to them while interpreting your dream.

You are the Expert!

You now have a number of dreams written down. When you are starting out, you may use a dream dictionary, which will help you identify the meaning behind every element in your dream. But you have to remember that you know yourself better than anyone else. So, let your subconscious guide you to help you understand and interpret your dreams. You will gain a lot of information about the memories stored in your unconscious.

By using the different guidelines discussed in this section, you can get a better understanding of yourself and the reasons for your dreams.

Chapter Two: Lucid Dreaming

Have you ever had a dream where you were a wizard or a bird? Have you dreamt that you were soaring through the clouds and shooting across the sky like Superman? Have you ever imagined a vacation on a Caribbean island? Remember any dream that ranks as one of your favorites; did you find it any less enjoyable because it was a dream? No, you enjoyed every bit of it. Now. how would you feel if you could control your dreams?

As mentioned in the earlier chapters, lucid dreaming is the method by which an individual is aware that he is dreaming. If a person is in a lucid dream, he can exercise the power of the dream. He can change the direction of the dream and also change the objects and entities in the dream. For instance, if you are in a lucid dream, and your environment is your bedroom, you can make your bed fly. You can create an entirely different universe behind the door to your bedroom. It is like you are writing your very own comic book. You can create your very own stage in your dreams and rehearse for a play or for a confrontation that you might have the next day.

History of Lucid Dreaming

The ancient practice of Yoga Nidra helps dreamers become more aware of what they are dreaming. This was a common practice of various people following Buddhist traditions. Some texts also show that lucid dreaming was a technique practiced in ancient Greece. For instance, Aristotle, the famous Greek philosopher, said, "Often when one is asleep, there is something in consciousness which declares that what then presents itself is but a dream." It was also believed that Galen, a physician from Pergamon, asked his patients to use this technique to help them overcome different problems and situations in life.

Lucid dreaming dates as far back as 415 AD. Researchers found the mention of Doctor Gennadius, a dreamer, in a letter written by Saint Augustine that talks about lucid dreaming.

Sir Thomas Browne, a famous physician, and philosopher also did his best to understand dreams since they fascinated him. He also tried the technique of lucid dreaming and penned down his learnings in the book Religio Medici. He stated that "...yet in one dream I can compose a whole Comedy, behold the action, apprehend the jests and laugh myself awake at the conceits thereof."

Another famous philosopher, Samuel Pepys, wrote in his dream diary, "I had my Lady Castlemayne in my arms and was admitted to use all the dalliance I desired with her and then dreamt that this could not be awake, but that it was only a dream."

Marie-Jean-Léon, the Marquis d'Hervey de Saint Denys, published his book, "Les Rêves et Les Moyens de Les Diriger, Observations Pratiques ('Dreams and the ways to direct them; practical observations')" anonymously. It was in this book that he described the technique and also how he felt when he employed this technique in his dreams. He also stated that people could wake up in their dreams and learn to change the way they respond to various situations in the dream. He was known as the father of lucid dreaming.

Frederik (Willem) van Eeden, a Dutch writer and psychiatrist, wrote an article, "A Study of Dreams," wherein he talked about lucid dreaming; it was in this article that he coined this term. Some psychologists consider "lucid dreaming" a misnomer, since they believe van Eeden was talking about something different from a lucid dream. Judging from his other works, van Eeden wanted people to have more control over their dreams, and therefore he used the word "lucid".

Benefits of Lucid Dreaming

Now that you know what lucid dreaming is, let us look at some benefits of this technique.

You Become More Aware

According to the Merriam Webster dictionary, lucidity is being more aware. It is only when you extend awareness into your dream state that you become aware of every event or situation taking place in your dream. It is important to understand that this awareness is only a reflection of your sensitivity to the various memories and thoughts in your mind. When you are aware of what happens in your dreams, you become aware of the different information stored in your brain. Lucid dreaming is a technique where you manifest your awareness in both your subconscious and conscious minds. There is a lot that you can improve when you are more aware of this information.

Most people are lost in their emotions and thoughts throughout the day, and they tend to act based on them. This is exactly what happens when you are lost in a dream. When you are lucid during a dream, you begin to focus on various aspects of your dream and relate them to the thoughts and emotions stored in your subconscious mind. This is a significant shift in your thought process since you no longer react to a situation based on your emotions or thoughts but relate to them directly because of your cognition.

You Are In Better Control

When you are aware of everything that happens in your mind, you do not succumb to your emotions and thoughts. This technique is not only about controlling everything that happens in your dream, but it actually is about learning to control how you respond to various situations. When you have this control, you can control your responses and react responsibly to your thoughts and emotions. You no longer react instantly to any situation but can focus on various aspects of the situation before you respond to them. This is a better way for you to deal with challenging situations in life.

Preventing Nightmares

When you use this technique during a nightmare, you can tell yourself that it is only a bad dream and not something happening in reality. You can also change the dream, so that it is no longer a nightmare. If you are unable to do the latter, you can challenge yourself and change the way you relate to the various situations happening in the dream. You can only do this since you know the dream is not real.

You Become More Creative

When you have lucid dreams, you can control how the dream progresses. When you are more aware of a dream, you can look for different ways to change the dream. This helps to explore how powerful your mind is and how you can use it to help you change your situation. If a dog is chasing you in your dream, you can change it to a puppy. You can also change the situation where the dog is no longer chasing you but only sniffing you, and you can pet him.

Lucid dreaming helps you change the way you think. You can take what you learn from your lucid dreams and apply it to your everyday life. You soon learn how to change negative emotions or thoughts into good ones. You can also learn to change your mood, so you are more cheerful and happy since you finally know that you create your experiences.

You Have Powerful Choices

When you have lucid dreams, you learn that you have a choice about how you want to deal with your thoughts and emotions. You can choose to witness your dreams, where you let the dream unfold but do not change any aspect of it, or you can change some parts of it. The former is like watching a film, while the latter allows you to change the ending of the film. Regardless of what you choose to do, you will learn that you have a choice. Once you know this, you know you can choose how to respond to various situations. Do you find yourself getting mad at someone at work or at home? Well, you are choosing to feel that. You can change the way you respond to the situation, change the way you relate to things, control your thoughts and emotions, and finally control your life.

Through lucid dreaming, you can determine the way you work with your emotions and thoughts. This technique helps you understand that you constantly work with your mind. You can change the way you respond to various situations in your life when you learn to work with similar situations in your dreams. You can use the insights or learnings from lucid dreaming, applying them to everyday situations in your life. It is only when you learn to focus on your dreams that you learn to be in a more awake state in life.

Chapter Three: Lucid Dreaming and Astral Projection

Most people tend to use astral production and lucid dreaming interchangeably since they believe they are the same thing. It is important to understand that these two are completely different phenomena or experiences. The most important difference between the two is that lucid dreaming only happens in a dream, while astral projection happens in the astral world, which is a dimension that is not a part of the physical world. Another difference to note is that astral projection is considered to be a real experience while lucid dreaming is not. The latter is only a phenomenon where you are more aware of what is happening in the dream, while the former is where the person experiences his consciousness in the astral realm.

When you try astral projection, you separate your consciousness from your physical body. Your consciousness then travels to a different plane where your astral body resides. It is never easy to do something like this, and it is for this reason most practitioners use specific beats, known as binaural beats, to help them ease into this projection.

What you must understand is that there is already an astral plane. Your consciousness is only visiting that plane, and thus, you cannot change or manipulate anything in that environment. You can also not change the way other people react or behave in that plane. Most people believe that astral projections are similar to near-death experiences since your soul leaves the body to move to a different dimension. People who practice astral projection often find themselves looking down at their physical bodies. Some people experience this phenomenon when they find themselves in near-death situations.

If you want to understand these experiences better, it is important to learn the fundamental differences between the phenomena.

In lucid dreaming,
- You only experience a dream
- You are not conscious
- You can be wherever you want to be (for example, the ocean, your childhood home, desert, etc.)
- You can change everything in your dream, including the characters and the environment
- Your soul or consciousness does not leave the body
- At the end of the experience, you find yourself awake

In astral projection,
- You are wide awake, and you separate or project your soul from your physical body
- The experience starts where you are currently (for example, your bedroom, office, living room, the park, etc.)
- Your body no longer has a consciousness since you have separated it from the body
- You can never change the way other people or inhabitants in the astral plane react to a situation
- It is easy to manipulate certain parts of this environment
- When you want to finish or end the astral projection, your consciousness returns to the physical body

Is Lucid Dreaming Necessary for Astral Projection?

You do not have to learn the technique of lucid dreaming if you want to project your consciousness from your physical body. You can learn how to project your consciousness from your body without learning how to maintain lucidity in a dream. Many people can separate their consciousness from their body by simply laying down on their bed. When you learn astral projection, you can project your consciousness from your body in the movie theater, at a restaurant, or even when you are at work. That being said, if you can maintain lucidity in a dream, it becomes easier for you to learn how to project your consciousness.

As mentioned earlier, some people can project their consciousness by simply lying down on the bed and closing their eyes. Others may have done this without realizing that they are projecting their consciousness out of their body, and they may be afraid that they have died. They may stand next to their body and wonder what happened to them. This is a strange situation to be in, but you can force your consciousness to move back into your body. The fear of death will naturally incline you do this.

Using Lucid Dreaming to Start Astral Projection

It is very difficult to master the art of lucid dreaming. If you want to maintain awareness or lucidity in a dream, you must ensure that you make your mind up even when you are asleep. This is something you must develop if you want to consciously project your consciousness into the astral plane. If you want to separate your consciousness from your physical body, you must learn how to move your consciousness or push it out from your physical body. It is only when you push it out that you can move it into the astral vehicle, which is also known as the astral body. When you separate your consciousness from your physical body, you push it into your astral or ghostly body. When you master lucid dreaming, you learn to keep your mind active and aware even when your body is sleeping.

What is Astral Projection?

The easiest way to separate your consciousness from your physical body is to learn how lucid dreaming works. This book will help you learn various aspects of lucid dreaming and what you can do to ease into it. Once you master this technique, use this as the foundation to help with astral projection. When you begin to focus on astral projection during lucid dreaming, you may find yourself paralyzed for a few seconds or minutes when you wake up. Your body only does this to protect you in your waking life, and help your mind determine whether you are in a dream or in a waking state. When your body is in this state, you should try to stretch or push your astral body away from your physical body. When you do this, you will feel like your consciousness or soul is moving away from your body. Do not be afraid when this happens, since this is how your body should react.

Let us understand astral projection using an analogy. During winter, you leave home wearing multiple layers of clothing and thermals that cling to your body for warmth. When you come back home, you remove layers of clothes and finally stretch out of the thermals. When you try astral projection, you notice that your consciousness is trying to stretch away from your physical body, much like the thermals.

Many people believe it is easy for them to cast their awareness or consciousness out of their bodies. They think they can have dual consciousness, and simply get out or move out of their physical body, but this is not what happens. If you successfully project your soul or consciousness from your physical body and look back at where you were a few moments ago, you see that your body is still on the couch or bed. You do not feel like you are still lying down, or that you are in a dream. You are finally awake and are standing next to your bed.

When you find yourself in this situation, you cannot feel your head on the pillow. You only see your body in that position. If someone were to tug or pull your arm, you could feel this even when you have projected your consciousness from your body. Your body has a cord that connects it to your soul or astral projection, and it uses this to ensure you return safely to your body. Your body will want to pull your consciousness or soul back into it quickly when you go astral the first few times.

When you go astral, try to push your soul as far away from your body as you can, so that your body cannot tug the soul back to it. If you are ready to go back into your body, you should only focus on that thought, and your body will tug the soul back into it. If you find yourself in terrible situations, you can use the help of spirits to guide you back into your body.

Some Things You Need to Know

There are times when you have may have a lucid dream, followed by a sense or feeling that you are separating your consciousness from your physical body. You must understand that this is not an astral projection. This is only a dream. If George Clooney or Julia Roberts is in your astral projection, you must remember you are dreaming. There are times when you may not fully move out of your body even when you have an astral projection, and this can be very frustrating. If your thoughts are not strong enough, and you cannot focus on pushing your consciousness from your body, you may move very quickly into a lucid dream. This is not an astral projection, even though it may be a great experience.

Some people feel they have experienced astral projection but not by leaving their bodies. What happens is that you can make your body vibrate at a different frequency that makes it easier for you to feel the astral plane, but your astral body does not stretch. This may have happened to many people who tried astral projection. You are in the astral plane, but your consciousness is not going anywhere; it is plugged into your physical body. When you do this, you may attract some negative emotions, entities, or thoughts that will suck your energy away, and this is something you do not want.

In other cases, you may find it easy to separate your soul or astral body from your physical body, taking the help of some energies or entities. If you know someone who can project his soul or consciousness from his body, ask him to help you through the process. It is a very tricky technique, and you need to have some training or help.

Chapter Four: Lucid Dreaming and Shamanic Journeying

The definitions of shamanic journeying and lucid dreaming vary depending on culture, and sometimes on resistance based on personal experiences. As you read earlier, the concepts and techniques of lucid dreaming came into existence thousands of years ago. Many indigenous cultures still use the concept of lucid dreaming as a form of therapy and practice it regularly. Experts believe that lucid dreaming is a form of shamanic therapy, a method used by soothsayers, healers, and medicine men to access energies, information, and insight. This means that lucid dreaming is not a fundamental concept by itself, but the technology or foundation of various shamanic methods.

The Conquerors of Consciousness

This is extremely different from how people today learn about lucid dreaming. People are now told that lucid dreaming is only a technique used when they want to indulge their fantasies, seek pleasure, or entertain themselves. There is nothing wrong with this definition of lucid dreaming, but this is a very limited definition. Many companies that manufacture lucid dreaming machines often use this definition to attract customers to boost their sales. They tell people they can seek pleasure through lucid dreaming, and this makes people purchase those machines to satiate their cravings.

It is unfortunate that people believe they can achieve whatever they want in their dreams, since it is only a dream, after all. The objective of any business working in this industry is to tap the ego of the buyer. According to Western civilization, it is our noble right to seize everything we want, because our desires matter the most. People are selfish, and when they fantasize about their dreams, they find a way to soothe their egos. They use their dreams to achieve everything they want but cannot achieve in real life.

Many people believe that a dream is a forest waiting to be plundered. Those who believe that their dreams have some meaning find it easier to use that meaning in their waking life. Sigmund Freud believed that people used dream interpretation only to satisfy or soothe their ego. Carl Jung, however, stated that people could drill into their subconscious mind during their dreams, even though this can hurt their conscious mind.

The objective of a lucid dreaming technique is to explore your dream, manipulate or change the dream, and conquer your thoughts and emotions. Lucid dreaming places you, the dreamer, at the center of your dream. Since you are the creator of your landscape, you can change everything about it. You conquer your consciousness and strike a balance between your subconscious and conscious minds.

The Negative Effects of Lucid Dreaming

The movie "The Men Who Stare at Goats" loosely represents some of the principles we have discussed, portraying a scenario in which the U.S. military tried to develop psi-based remote viewing to identify or detect targets. The movie "Inception" portrays a scenario in which the military assigned a task force to identify locations, targets, and people using lucid dreaming.

All of this work was once classified but is now available in the US Military database. It was in 1995 that the U.S. military decided there was no way remote viewing could be used to achieve the best results. Various programs, such as Gondala Wish, Sunstreak, and Stargate, did have some success with remote viewing. Dale Graff, the previous chief of Stargate, explained the process in his book "Tracks in the Psychic Wilderness," and mentioned how the team located a Russian airplane using remote viewing.

This means you need to be consistent with your practice if you want to maintain lucidity when you dream. You need to have an active imagination, but do not have to work with any higher power or energy. Shamanism is a different practice since the healers and medicine men use different energies and powers to compete with each other. They also use different spells and herbs. Lucid dreaming is not very different from Shamanism. Robert Waggoner, a psychotherapist, pointed out that one can use lucid dreaming to intrude into others' dreams, and no machine or tool is needed to do this.

The Emergence of Spirituality

Most people believe lucid dreams are used to stabilize the dreamer's hold on the dream. Lucid dreams, however, can also destabilize the dreamer's hold, and there are times when the dream can open doors to other worlds. You cannot prevent a nightmare from being uncontrollably bad, even if you maintain lucidity during your dream. When you confront these dark spirits and focus on your unconscious mind, you can unleash your spirituality. The American Psychiatric Association has listed spiritual emergence as a diagnostic category and claims it can lead to both spiritual and existential distress if not monitored correctly. You may have such dreams when you are under stress or duress, and also when you are unsure of where life will take you when you move from one role to another. Scott Sparrow, a psychotherapist, stated that the fear some people experience when they have lucid dreams helps them control their dreams, and therefore it is a necessary adversary.

Many people have had terrible cramping and other physical ailments after they practice lucid dreaming. Metaphorically, you can say that these people had trouble digesting their lucid dreams, and therefore felt pain. Ken Kelzer, a psychotherapist and lucid dreamer, also talks about his negative psychological and physical symptoms after lucid dreaming. He detailed his experiences in his book, "The Sun and the Shadow." If you are serious about lucid dreaming, you should do your best to ensure you create the right setting and environment for your dream sessions.

Ask yourself the following questions:
- Is the space I am working in safe for this practice?
- Is there a specific time when I should practice lucid dreaming?
- Can I ask someone to help me through this practice?

How to Initiate Yourself

By now, you may have gathered that lucid dreaming is not easy, and when you let yourself become aware that you are in a dream, you must learn to strike a balance between the control you can exercise and your awareness. This is the only way you can truly meet the various forces and entities in the spirit realm. It is best to look at your dream like a private initiation.

Some people also have terrible dreams wherein they find themselves lucid. They may dream about death, pain, and sorrow, and may see dead bodies, demons, ghosts, or fire. These are analogous to different initiation dreams that people have when they practice shamanic rituals. Ethnographers believe that these dreams help an individual express his essence and helps the person connect with various other energies in the world. The following is an example of a lucid dream taken from the book, "Sleep Paralysis: A Dreamer's Guide."

"I was reading when I noticed that the wall (about 6 feet from the end of my bed) started to sort of wobble. My body was paralyzed, unable to move. My breathing was kind of non-existent, though I desperately needed more air. Suddenly, it opened up into a black void, like a 9 feet black hole, vaguely the shape of a figure. "O my God," I thought, "I am dreaming. This can't be true." The black hole oozed into the room. I was beyond terror. I still don't understand how my heart didn't collapse. The blackness started molding itself into a recognizable shape. It became a 9 ft tall Japanese devil or devilish-looking Samurai. Viciously grinning, he said, "You are not dreaming. You thought you could 'integrate me.'" He then, in one sweeping movement, stretched out his enormous black hand, grabbed me, stuffed me into his blood-red mouth, and swallowed me. Then I fell into unconsciousness for a moment; now, a vortex pulled me down into an abyss of no dimensions. All of a sudden, I was spat back out into his hand. Somehow, I had crystallized into a red ruby. I WAS a ruby; I felt like a ruby. So, there I was, in the big hand of a giant, looking at him, and he is looking at me. In that moment of seeing each other, something happened. We looked at each other, became truly aware of each other, and then, there was love. I know what the mystics talk about/can't talk about. There is believing, and then, there is knowing."

If you read the initiation dream carefully, you know the demon in the dream scoffed at the individual's paradigm. James Hillman, a depth psychologist, suggested that your dream figure is not only a representation of who you are. It is a representation of your entire being. In the above dream, the dreamer surrendered herself to the demon and died. She fell into an abyss and was reborn with a new understanding of life.

The Revolution of Lucid Dreaming

People often use dream control as a means to surrender. This helps them learn to live in the present and go with the flow. Most people use the tension between working with the unknown and maintaining awareness in a dream to help them connect to their subconscious mind. This helps them maintain lucidity for longer periods in their dreams. It is of utmost importance now for dreamers to tap into the energy and wisdom of our ancestors to understand various events taking place in the world. This wisdom can help us understand our communities better and help us assess the effects of the economy on the environment and civilization.

Lee Irwin, a famous anthropologist, talked about how waking visions and big dreams integrated with opposing worldviews and conflicting paradigms during the clash between the West and the Native Americans in the seventeenth, eighteenth, and nineteenth centuries. This clash led to the rise of leaders who were both healers and visionaries who could lead forces against the colonial West. Barbara Tedlock, an anthropologist, talked about the effect of dreams on the Mayan civilization during the civil war in Guatemala in the 1980s. People within these communities were led by dreamers and visionaries who found a way to preserve their traditions while they accepted new cultures. These communities participated in the economy while they continued to follow their culture and faith.

That being said, you cannot succeed only because you have a dream. You can use the power of these dreams to help you create a template, making it easier for you to survive against all the odds. People now know their limitations in the current world, but they are still unaware of the destructive power of the world. We can use the power of dreams to prevent destruction, but to do this, we must be open to remembering them, sharing them with the world, and acting upon our dreams with hearts and eyes wide open.

Chapter Five: Preparation for Learning Lucid Dreaming

Most beginners have many questions about lucid dreaming, and this chapter answers some of those questions. You can use the information in this chapter to prepare yourself for a lucid dreaming experience.

When can I have my first lucid dream?

Experts believe that beginners can have their first lucid dream anywhere between three and thirty days from starting a lucid-dreaming program. This is dependent on their focus and how well they follow all the instructions to help them practice mindfulness. This book is only a guide, and there are some people who already have the necessary skills to help them become aware of their dream on their first attempt. Some may take months or years to develop this skill, and if you are not fully committed to it, you may take longer. Ask yourself the following questions if you are unable to have your first lucid dream:

- Do I spend enough time every morning to write down my dreams?
- Do I meditate for at least ten minutes every day?

- Am I doing everything in my power to improve my self-awareness every day?
- Do I perform enough reality checks each day? How frequently do I perform these checks?
- Did I develop a plan for what I want to do in my first lucid dream?
- Am I planting various ideas for my lucid dream in my subconscious mind?
- Have I learned the right techniques?

Can lucid dreams harm me?

You are not going to be in any physical danger, but you should be prepared to feel differently. You also need to ensure you are open to having new experiences. None of these experiences can hurt you, but you may find some of them a little odd.

Can I switch to a lucid state as a beginner?

Practice makes perfect, but most people experience a lucid dream in a few nights. You can use different techniques given in the book to help you maintain lucidity in your dream.

Can I have nightmares in a lucid state?

You can have a good or bad dream when you sleep, and you can be lucid in either of those dreams. The only difference is that you may be in an unpleasant dream. If you maintain lucidity, you can play an active role in controlling this situation, as you have a clear understanding of the situation you are in. It is only when you do this that you can confront the thoughts and images giving you this nightmare.

Are there signs to help me know I'm lucid?

If you use dreams to initiate lucid dreaming, you become aware or lucid when you know you are dreaming. If you have watched movies, you know that some characters realize they are dreaming, but they do not know how to control various aspects of that dream. They may scream or jerk awake, and may not even remember what they were dreaming about. You must understand that this is not lucid dreaming.

Lucid dreaming has very different effects on your life. When you are aware that you are dreaming and you say that out loud, a certain clarity of thought rushes into your mind. You begin to focus on every aspect of your dream and are more aware of your body. Lucid dreaming is much like a waking experience, and it is only when you feel this way that you can take in a lot of information from your surroundings.

Your dreams often have different features, and it is easy for these features to change even when you have lucid dreams. For example, you may be playing with puppies, and these puppies can change into boxes or clothes. You can, however, go back to playing with puppies if you maintain lucidity. These subtle changes cannot be controlled even when you remain lucid during a dream. Your subconscious mind plays an important role in this.

Can I remain lucid for longer?

Most lucid dreamers, especially beginners, cannot control the length of their lucid dreams. They may be too excited in their dream, and this wakes their physical body. There are times when you may forget you are lucid in a dream, and your subconscious mind may take control over everything in your dream. When this happens, it becomes a regular dream since you no longer have control. If you want to dream for longer, you should learn to stay focused and calm when you dream. You should learn to stay grounded mentally and tell yourself that you are only dreaming.

One of the easiest ways to stay lucid in your dreams for longer is to perform reality checks. You can either say, "I am dreaming", out loud, or walk around. This energy will stimulate your mind and keep it active. You can also make your conscious mind focus on your dream body and avoid looking at your physical body. If you follow these techniques, you can experience a lucid dream for as long as 60 minutes.

Can I add more elements and colors to the scenery?

It is difficult, especially if you are a beginner, for you to change the dream scene. One of the main reasons why this happens is that you don't think this can happen in your dream. Since you are a beginner, you do not understand how to control your dreams, which makes it hard for you to change anything about your dream.

The best way to help you understand the limits of your control is to work with your subconscious mind to understand your dream's logic. You can do the following to change some aspects of the scenery:

- Walk around in your dream and find the door. Visualize that you will move to a different world when you walk through this door.
- If you have lakes or other water bodies in your scenery, think about them as portals and jump in.
- You can also use a mirror portal to move from your current dream world into another.
- If you are watching a movie or TV series, change the scene and jump into it. You will see the world around you become 3-dimensional.
- Look away from the current dream scene and imagine a change in the scene. When you finally turn around, you will see a whole new world.

There are many things you can do if the only trouble is creativity. You must remember that your consciousness plays a significant role when it comes to your dreams. If you are unsure of your strengths and constantly wonder if you can change the different aspects of your dreams, your confidence may falter. If you learn from your mistakes and experiences and remain confident, you will learn there are many things you can do when you dream.

Can I dream that I am flying?

Most people want to learn how to fly when they have lucid dreams. They often want to master this art before they do anything else. Having said that, if you are new to lucid dreaming, you must avoid this since the concept is slightly difficult to grasp. Some people are lucky, and they take off like Superman while there are others who may bump into buildings, some who cannot get off the ground because of gravity, and others who get stuck on clotheslines.

Let us take the example of the movie "The Matrix". When Neo and Morpheus fight in the virtual world, the former beat the latter easily. Why do you think Neo was better? Was it because he was smarter, fitter, or stronger? No, all it took him was a little confidence. He believed he was better than Morpheus, and this belief helped him win the fight.

The same idea works with lucid dreams as well. You need to learn the art of flying when you have lucid dreams. This makes it easier for you to fly when you master maintaining lucidity in later dreams.

Can lucid dreams cause fatigue?

This is another myth. People dream during their REM sleep, and they may dream for over ninety minutes. An experienced lucid dreamer may have at least three lucid dreams in a week, and each dream may last for at least fifteen minutes. Some people believe this is like lost sleep because their mind is not quite at rest, but this is not too much time at all. Lucid dreams can give you a natural high, which leaves you with extra energy throughout the day. Some people experience lucid dreaming every night, in each of their sleep cycles. This means a lucid dream is not restricted only to their REM sleep. They have only had lucid dreams, and they have never complained about their lack of energy.

Some people choose to have normal dreams, and they let go of their lucidity when they have nothing else to add to their dream. There are others who choose to snap out of their lucid state. They wake up and open their eyes before they go back to bed. A very small number of people have had trouble with their dreams and are unable to sleep without any disturbances. This does make them feel a little sleep deprived throughout the day.

If you experience lucid dreaming naturally, but are afraid of the intensity of your dreams, visit a doctor or specialist. You must remember that anything in excess is bad for your body and mind, and there is a way to snap out of lucidity.

Can I be stuck in the dreamscape?

Do you think you can get stuck in a lucid dream the same way a child may get hung up on a painting or horror movie? If this is the case, remember it is not possible, since it is only a dream and not your reality. You cannot get stuck in a lucid dream, much like how you cannot get stuck in a nightmare or a regular dream. Only movies use this as a plot. When you are lucid dreaming, you can choose to wake up when you desire. Most people begin lucid dreaming when they use it as a means to wake up from bad dreams or nightmares. They can close their dream eyes and yell at their mind to wake up. You can also use these moments to help you switch to a guided dream from a nightmare. It is possible for you to become engrossed in a false awakening state or lucid nightmare. This is, however, not like being trapped forever in a dream. These states are both enlightening and frightening, and they have the same length as your REM sleep.

Do my dreams represent my psychic abilities?

Most people are under the misconception that their dreams represent their underlying psychic abilities. What is most important to understand is that nothing becomes real, simply because you want it to. If this were the case, everybody would win $1,000,000 or look exactly how they want to. There is little or no research that shows that dreams have psychic capabilities. People have heard of a friend who may have had this amazing psychic dream, so there is a possibility that such dreams are real. You must bear in mind that some stories are fabricated, and there may be some coincidences.

Can I communicate with my subconscious?

It is important to remember that your dreams are memories, emotions, and thoughts taken from your subconscious mind. This means there is two-way communication between your subconscious and conscious minds. One of the easiest ways to do this is to communicate with yourself in the dream. You can ask yourself some questions to communicate with your subconscious. This helps you strengthen the connection between your subconscious and conscious minds.

Do I die in real life if I die in a lucid dream?

This is untrue, and research shows that lucid dreams do not have a direct impact on your body. You may be chased by a dog, hurt yourself, or even die in a lucid dream. There are times when you may have fallen from a tower or the topmost floor of a building. This does not mean you died in reality. When you wake up, you realize that it was a dream, and it obviously did not kill you.

Can I have false awakenings?

A false awakening is a situation where you still are asleep, but your body believes you are awake. This is a very different state of mind, and you may have some vivid experiences similar to lucid dreams. Some people get out of bed, get dressed, grab a quick breakfast, and ride to work even in their false awakening state. They can perform such actions since they are in autopilot mode. This means that the experience is not fun and cannot be controlled. Having said that, the realism is quite shocking, which is why most people do not realize when they are in a false awakening state.

Lucid dreamers often have more experiences with false awakening than other people, and this is due to a clash between their consciousness and the dream world. It is an odd side effect of lucid dreaming but is not dangerous. This phenomenon can also lead to the development of dreams in the waking state, known as conscious dreams. Many movies have used false awakenings as a part of the plot to help viewers understand the characters' fears. One of the easiest ways to identify a false awakening is to check whether you are in a dream state or reality.

Can I use machines?

There are many machines you can use to help you with lucid dreaming, such as REM Dreamer, DreamMask and NovaDreamer. These machines use various lucidity triggers, and your subconscious mind uses these triggers in your dream. It is your job to focus on these triggers or cues, to help you understand or become more aware of yourself in the dream. These machines do not ensure that you remain lucid during your dreams, but when you use them correctly, you can improve the chances of staying lucid. These machines can also shift your consciousness from your physical body into the dreamscape.

How do I use brainwave music or messages?

Brain wave music or messaging is one of the easiest ways to shift from the waking state to a meditative state. This entertainment uses precision audio technology which stimulates the brain to move into a deeply meditative, calm, and relaxed state. This form of entertainment is good for the following reasons:

- This entertainment helps you switch from the waking state to a meditative state immediately, and improves your visualization and self-awareness, thereby helping you stay conscious and aware of yourself in different states.

- This form of entertainment also helps you enter the BAMA, or Body Asleep/Mind Awake state, and this is one of the best ways to have a lucid dream. You can also have an out of body experience when you are in this state. When you are in this state, your mind works hard to ensure that your body is in the dream state and asleep.

Are dream herbs good?

You can use dream herbs at times if you want to improve the intensity of your dreams. Some herbs also help you recall your dreams better. There are times when you may have meaningful, vivid, and insightful dreams when you take dream herbs. Some experts recommend herbs if you want to create or have interesting experiences in your dreams. You can also experiment with them to learn more about your mind, how you react to dreams, and, sometimes, just for fun.

Can I induce out of body experiences (OBE) using lucid dreams?

We discussed out of body experiences, also known as astral projections, in the third chapter of the book. Lucid dreaming can induce an out of body experience. There are times when you may have unexplained or unimaginable experiences even when you practice lucid dreaming techniques. There may be times when you feel like your consciousness is exiting your body when you have a lucid dream. This is probably only a transition your consciousness is making when it moves from your physical body to the dream or imaginary body. This experience is like a false awakening.

Chapter Six: Preparing for a Lucid Dream Experience

Most people wonder how quickly they can have lucid dreams, and what most people do not know is that you can have a lucid dream the day you read about it. You can have a lucid dream within the first few nights of your initial attempt, since the only thing you have to do focus on your dream reality. This means you must become aware of your dream, but this is easier said than done.

Some people are not as lucky, and some may even take a month before they experience a lucid dream. The timeline varies between individuals, but some people only need to focus in the right direction for them to have lucid dreams. Having said that, you should not worry if you are unable to have a lucid dream the night you finish reading this book. It may take you some time to prepare yourself mentally and physically before you have a lucid dream. When you use the various techniques mentioned in this book, you will know exactly what you need to do to have lucid dreams. There will come a day when you do not have to put in so much effort to have a lucid dream. All you will need to do is focus on a thought or picture while you go to sleep and know that you will dream about that at night.

This chapter focuses on some tips and strategies you can use to experience lucid dreams. Before we dive into these methods, let us establish your goals.

Understand Your Goals

You must do the following when you learn various lucid dreaming techniques.

- Increase your chances of recalling your dreams. Since you dream for at least 100 minutes every night, pay attention to everything happening in your dream.
- Make sure you focus on different aspects of your dreams, such as sounds, sensations, sights, and feelings.
- Focus on your thoughts and learn to recognize when you are dreaming. This means you must learn to differentiate between dreams and reality. You can do this easily using reality checks, and we will cover these in detail in this chapter.
- Learn to become more aware of your life, so you become more aware of your dreams.
- Push your mind into becoming more aware when you have dreams. This is the only way you can have more lucid dreams.
- Learn visualization skills to help you manifest your dream. You can also visualize being in a lucid dream.
- Learn to focus on the content of your dream before you go to bed. We will look at this technique in detail later in the chapter.

When you incorporate the objectives mentioned above in your life, you can have lucid dreams every night. You must understand that your dreams only reflect the memories, thoughts, emotions, and experiences you have during your waking life. It is for this reason you can have a lucid dream by just thinking about something that transpired during the day.

Tips and Techniques

Learn

When you want to develop a skill, you must learn everything about that skill. This book has all the information you need about lucid dreaming, but there are tons of articles and videos out there to help you further in your journey.

Use Checks

I am sure you know what a reality check is. You should perform at least two dozen reality checks every day, especially at the beginning. You can decrease the number of reality checks you perform as you improve and develop your skills. These reality checks do not take more than a few seconds to perform. Consider the following example:

- Look at your hands.
- If there is a wall next to you, try to push your palms through the wall.
- If you are in a dream, your hand will go through the wall, but if you are not, your palms touch the surface of the wall.

The objective of a reality check is to help you determine whether you are asleep or awake. The outcome of any activity you perform will be different depending on your state. When you repeat such an action numerous times every day, it becomes muscle memory. Therefore, when you are dreaming, you can either perform the same reality check or use any other technique to determine if you are in a dream. This will help activate the part of your mind that focuses on various aspects of the dream, thereby inducing lucidity.

Reduce Screen Time

You should turn off every device, such as mobile phones, laptops, tablets, televisions, Kindles, etc., at least an hour before you go to bed. Turn off all the lights in your room, so you encourage your body and mind to go to sleep. This is the only way your brain releases enough melatonin to force your body to go to sleep. Keep your environment dark since light affects the production of melatonin.

Use Alarms

Most beginners get this step wrong when they start learning about lucid dreaming. If you follow the steps mentioned in this section carefully, you can improve. You should set the alarm to go off at least five hours after you go to bed. The objective is to bring you out of your REM sleep. You will, however, go right back to sleep using the methods mentioned in the next few steps and return to a state of lucid dreaming. If you want to succeed at using this method, keep the following points in mind:

- Keep your eyes shut when you try to turn off the alarm. Make sure your phone or clock is close to you, so you can reach it without having to open your eyes.
- Do not use a blaring sound as the alarm. Yes, the alarm should wake you up, but when you use buzzing sounds, your mind and body become active, making it difficult for you to go back to a state of lucid dreaming. Therefore, use something pleasant as the alarm.

Do Not Open Your Eyes

It is extremely important to do this, especially when you wake up from a dream. You must keep your eyes closed, so you convince your body to go back to sleep. Your mind, however, should be slightly awake.

Use WBTB

Wake Back to Bed, or WBTB is a method you use to train your body to go back to sleep even when your mind is alert. There may be times when you suddenly wake from sleep. It is during those times that you should learn to go back to sleep while your mind is still active, making it easier for you to maintain lucidity when you have a dream. This may sound impossible, but you can master this if you practice enough. We will look at this method in detail later in the book.

Meditate
In the previous sections, we looked at how important it is for you to separate your body and mind. If you practice meditation correctly, you can develop these skills. Buddhist monks are the best example here. They can meditate for as long as ten hours without taking a break. They forget about hunger and are not bothered by noises around them. They sit still, meaning they do not move even one muscle in their body. They are, however, looking at beautiful visions and experiencing everything that happens around them differently. You may wonder how you can achieve something as brilliant as this. They can do this since they have separated their mind from their body. Their bodies are in a position and state of rest, while their mind is active. Since lucid dreaming is similar to this, you must develop the same skill set.

Use Musical Aids
Many people use aids such as binaural beats and white noise to focus, concentrate, or sleep. These aids also help you when you want to experience lucid dreaming. The different frequencies being played in these musical aids always enter your ears at the same time. Your brain, however, still looks at these beats or music as a single frequency making it easier for you to focus or concentrate. There are numerous videos on YouTube with these tracks, or you can download an app that has a variety of music. If you want to use these for lucid dreaming, you must ensure that the frequency of this music matches the frequency of the brain waves that help you become aware during your dream. Experts recommend that you stick to music between the frequency 4 Hertz - 8 Hertz.

Play Games
When you play games such as *Counter-Strike* or *Age of Empires*, you are in a completely different world. You can explore and learn more about every aspect of this universe. If you play games such as *Defense of the Ancients* or *Dungeons and Dragons*, you may take up a role. Sometimes, you may want to take a different path to your teammates, just to see what's there. This is

what you must do when you sleep, too. When you find yourself in a different world, focus on various aspects of that world, and explore it. It becomes easier to do this in your dreams when you play video games in your waking life.

Take Galantamine

Most Alzheimer's patients are given this natural supplement to improve their memory and brain function. Galantamine is a plant-based substance found in plants such as spider lily and dandelions. The substance can be used orally. According to the study, "Exploring the Effects of Galantamine Paired with Meditation and Dream Reliving on Recalled Dreams: Toward an integrated protocol for lucid dream induction and nightmare resolution (2018)," this supplement improves the quality of sleep during your REM stage. It also lengthens your sleep, thereby making it easier for you to remember your dreams. The study also showed that people who took this supplement had a higher chance of experiencing a lucid dream than those who took placebos.

Take Supplements

Experts recommend that you take vitamin B6 supplements if you want to ease into lucid dreaming. There is limited research to determine the correlation between lucid dreaming and this vitamin, but according to the study, "Effects of Pyridoxine on Dreaming: A Preliminary Study (2002)," Vitamin B6 increases the serotonin levels in your body which makes your dreams more colorful. You may also have vivid dreams if you take these supplements, and this makes it easier to remember them the following morning.

Time

You must understand that it will take time for you to learn a new skill. Therefore, give yourself enough time to do the following:
- Maintain a journal wherein you write your dreams
- Meditate and visualize the dream during the day
- Maintain a routine before you go to bed
- Learn more about lucid dreaming
- Prepare yourself for bed

It is not recommended that you practice any lucid dreaming technique if you have a busy life. If you work every day or are a student, you have some time commitments that may make it hard for you to set some time out regularly to focus on these techniques. You should ideally spend at least thirty minutes every day to develop the necessary skills. Therefore, plan your day in advance, so you have sufficient time to practice lucid dreaming techniques.

Discipline

You must maintain a disciplined approach if you want to learn how to remain lucid when you dream, which is a little like learning a new sport or technical skill. It is only when you practice that you become a better player or coder. You may not achieve the expected results when you attempt to maintain lucidity in your dreams for the first few times. You are only laying the foundation to help you become more aware of your dreams in the future. If you are committed to your routine and techniques, you can get the most out of lucid dreaming. Therefore, you must be disciplined in your approach. You should be consistent with the various tips and techniques you use for at least thirty days.

Passion

Was there some task at work that you hated doing? Did you put in as much effort to complete this task as you did to complete your favorite tasks? The point of these questions is to help you understand that passion is what makes learning more fun. It is only when you are passionate about something that you are motivated to stick to the training. This is the only way you can maintain lucidity during your dreams.

Tips to Ease into a Lucid Dream

It may be extremely fun to have a lucid dream, but it is a difficult journey. The experience can also be daunting. Having said that, when you have a lucid dream, you could change your life for the better. We have looked at some of the benefits of lucid dreaming earlier in the book.

This is a skill you must develop, and like every other skill, it does take some time for you to become aware of being in a dream. There is no single way to do this, and there are numerous methods one can employ when they try to maintain lucidity during dreaming. This section lists some methods to help you begin your journey.

• Use a dream journal regularly and make a note of at least one dream after you wake up if you can remember them.

• Meditate for ten minutes every day, so you become aware of your thoughts and emotions.

• Look for different signs in your dreams to help you become more aware or lucid when you have dreams with similar signs.

• Ask yourself if you are dreaming. You can also perform a physical action to help you determine if you are dreaming or not.

• You can either use a spray with a relaxing aroma or fill your pillow with essences to calm your mind.

• Take some lucid dreaming pills; you want to increase the intensity or vividness of your dreams.

• If you wake up or jerk away when you have a dream, use the wake- induced lucid dreaming method to help you go back to sleep and continue to be aware of your dream.

• Purchase a good mattress, especially if you want to sleep well.

• When you drift off to sleep, focus on your surroundings, and observe any hallucinations that you may be having.

• You can induce lucid dreams through smells using aromatherapy. This form of lucid dreaming is known as Smell Induced Lucid Dreams.

• Observe the posture that works best for you. Relax into that posture before you go to bed.

- Experiment with different lucid dream techniques. We will cover some of these in detail later in the book.
- Use a lucid dreaming application to control your thoughts and emotions when you go to bed. You can download this on your laptop or phone.
- Watch a video before you go to bed, preferably a lucid dreaming video, so you motivate or stimulate your mind to become aware during a dream. Alternatively, you can also listen to subliminal messages or lucid dreaming hypnosis sessions.
- Use dream herbs to have memorable and vivid dreams.
- You can increase the intensity of your dreams by eating cheese before you go to bed.
- If you have trouble sleeping, especially during your REM cycle, visit a doctor, and find a way to get rid of these issues.
- When you are aware of a dream, you can also ask the dream to help you stay lucid when you have other dreams. This will stimulate your brain to remain conscious during all dreams.
- Visualize or manifest a plot that you want to see in your dream. You can use lucid dream movies to help you do this.
- Give yourself some time every day to daydream. This helps you explore various fantasies and realities.
- You can use mnemonic induction to help you have lucid dreams. Use this technique right before you go to bed. We will look at this technique in detail in the next chapter.
- If you are not very good at remembering dreams the following morning, you can set the alarm during your REM cycle. When you wake up, and if you have had a dream, write it down in your journal before you go back to sleep. Alternatively, you can also wear a digital watch that beeps every 60 minutes. You can use this beep to remind yourself to perform a reality check in your dream.
- Read more about Yoga Nidra.

- If you fall asleep in various locations, encourage your subconscious to have false awakenings.
- You can also use different methods to have out of body experiences, like astral projection.
- You can move into a lucid dream through sleep paralysis.
- If counting makes you sleep, count backward as you become drowsy. Say, "I am dreaming," before you move to the next number in the sequence.
- You can sleep during your day, especially after a workout.
- Relax every weekend, and practice the techniques mentioned in the book. This approach helps you determine the technique that works best for you.
- Most people are afraid of lucid dreams because they think it may harm their consciousness. This, however, is not true. All you must remember is that lucidity or awareness is a positive and powerful tool you can use to grow.
- Sleep for at least eight hours every night.
- You can meditate before you go to sleep or while you are sleeping.
- Use lucid dreams technology if you can afford it.

You can use different methods to make it easier for you to practice lucid dreaming. If this is overwhelming, remember this is only an overview of the various methods you can use. If you want to begin lucid dreaming tonight, use the following methods to become more aware during a dream.

Perform a Reality Check

When you dream, you must determine if you are actually in a dream. You can either stomp your foot or pluck a flower depending on where you are in your dream.

Visualize the Dream

You can plan what happens in your lucid dream. Focus on your desire, close your eyes, and visualize that thought or desire. You can also visualize and focus on being aware of your dream.

Repeat Your Steps

If you wake up in the middle of the night, repeat all the steps you performed before you went to bed. This helps you fall asleep easily.

Make sure you do not forget these tips. These techniques may sound a little weird or strange, and there are times when you may wonder why you are following them. It is normal to feel this way. You may not always get the right results when you use these techniques. Having said that, it is only when you master your basics that you can move on to the advanced techniques. When you have a lucid dream, you finally learn to differentiate between dreams and reality.

Since you are a beginner, it is important for you to maintain a routine so your consciousness remains lucid or aware during a dream.

Maintaining a Routine

This section gives you a basic routine you can use to ease into a lucid dream.

Meditation

There are times during the day when you are in a half-sleep state, and during these states, you may either feel drowsy or calm. When you feel this way, lie down on your bed or a couch and relax. Let your thoughts and emotions drift. The only thing you need to focus on is to force your body to fall asleep while you are conscious. To do this, focus on the thin cord that connects your body to your consciousness, and use the cord to push your mind away from your body. This is not only a very relaxing exercise but also creates hypnagogic sensations. You may see geometric patterns, feel as if you are floating, or view some dream impressions. Meditation is a great way to improve your visualization and awareness skills.

Journaling

If you want to lucid dream frequently, maintain a dream journal. Make a note of your dreams when you wake up every morning. Spend at least five minutes every morning to write down every dream you had. This not only makes it easier for you to recall your dreams but also helps you maintain lucidity when you dream. This step is extremely important, and therefore, you should not ignore it.

Planting an Idea

In this step, you can plant an idea or thought in your subconscious mind so that you dream about the idea later. This is nothing like inception since the idea is yours. One of the easiest ways to plant an idea in your subconscious mind is to visualize or fantasize about the character or plot during the day. Consider the following example: when you watch a horror movie, you constantly think about the demon or ghost chasing you. You also visualize shapes and other objects in the darkness, which can give you nightmares. You can use daydreams and happy thoughts to have good dreams, in the same way. These daydreams and happy thoughts will feature in your dream if they are visceral. Alternatively, you can also use the concept of visualization and manifestation to convince your mind that you will get lucid dreams tonight. If you make this thought the last thought of your day, you will definitely have a lucid dream.

You have turned your alarm off, so now close your eyes and begin to focus on the dream; this is where the magic begins. When you focus on your dream, your body soon begins to drift off to sleep. It will, however, test whether your mind is still awake. Your body may tell your brain that you need to curl, scratch your nose, pull the covers over your head, etc. Do not do this. When you do not move, your body believes that you are asleep. It will release control, and your unconscious mind takes over. You see shapes, colors, images, and scenic views, and all of these come together to create shapes and images. These will all come together and take some shape. When you are aware of these images and shapes, you are finally aware of your dreams.

Things to Do When you Are Aware

Now that you know what a lucid dream is, you must learn what to do when you become aware or are lucid in your dream. If you do not know what you must do, you may become too excited and wake up from your dream. Use the following techniques to help you stabilize the dream when you become aware that you are in a dream:

- Look at yourself and observe your movements
- Walk around and focus on how your feet feel on the ground
- Say something out loud
- Rub your palms together
- Feel the sensation of every movement when you walk or spin around in your dream

You cannot stay lucid in a dream if you do not use the right techniques. The techniques mentioned above stimulate your mind, which makes it easier for you to change your dream into reality. If you stimulate your mind and stabilize your presence or awareness in the dream, you can make this dream last longer.

Things to do in Your Dream

Once you learn to stabilize your thoughts and emotions in a lucid dream, you should also learn to calmly explore everything in the environment. You should never make changes to the dream or any aspect of it too soon. Do not do something too fancy, like teleporting yourself to the top of the Eiffel Tower, when you find yourself aware for the first time in your dream. If you do this, you may become too excited, and this may jerk you awake. When you start off with lucid dreaming, it is best for you to walk or float around, look at the environment, and soak in every object and aspect of that environment. You must still remember that your dream is only your virtual reality, and this is both living and tangible. This is the only way you can continue lucid dreaming.

Chapter Seven: 5 Lucid Dreaming Techniques

People have used different techniques to have lucid dreams. This chapter covers some of the simplest techniques approved by psychologists.

Dream Induced Lucid Dream (DILD)

As mentioned earlier, a dream induced lucid dream is one where you realize that you have a dream inside another dream. This method is beginner-friendly and easy. Most people who want to try lucid dreaming use this technique. The most important thing to remember about lucid dreaming is that you must be aware of or lucid in your dream. Some common techniques of DILD are:

All Day Awareness of ADA

When you are fully aware of yourself throughout the day, you can easily distinguish between your dream and the real world. You can use the various techniques mentioned above (reality checks) to help you become more aware of your dreams.

Using Checks

Most people never think they are dreaming since their mind always believes they are awake. When you decide to perform regular reality checks, you become more aware of the dream world and the real world. Your dreams become more clear and vivid when you improve your awareness.

Self-Hypnosis

Self-hypnosis is a state where you are relaxed. This technique is more like programming your mind to have a lucid dream.

Dream Signs

As mentioned earlier, a sign in your dream can be a cue that helps you determine if you are in a dream or not. When you pay attention to these cues and signs, you begin to notice them a lot more. This helps you have more lucidity in your dreams.

CAT or Cycle Adjustment Technique

Daniel Love was the one who created this technique, and there are three steps you should follow when you use this technique.

Step One

Set the alarm to at least sixty minutes before the usual time you wake up. You should do this every day for at least two weeks to help your body clock reset, because you may not have a lucid dream when you start off with this technique.

Step Two

After the fourteenth day, you can go back to your previous schedule, but wake up earlier every other day. This means you should follow the sequence: early, normal, early, normal. When you go to bed, let your body know that you want to wake up earlier than normal, and make sure to perform enough checks to determine whether you are asleep or awake. You should prepare yourself for the early morning before you go to bed each night.

You can sleep in on days when you wake up at your usual time, but avoid sleeping in for longer, so you do not disrupt your new cycle.

Step Three

Your body finally learns to wake up early and will expect your mind to do this, too. Since the body is active, it stimulates your mind, which in turn helps your mind retain consciousness even when you dream. This increases the chances of being lucid in a dream, and you may have lucid dreams at least four times every week.

So, what do you think you should do when you wake up earlier than usual? You can do almost anything, but ensure you do not go back to sleep. Keep performing reality checks every day and do it as often as possible when you wake up earlier than usual. This helps you stimulate your mind and keep it active throughout the day. You can then go about normally throughout your day. It is only when you do more reality checks that your mind can differentiate between a dream and reality.

WBTB

WBTB is an acronym for 'Wake Back to Bed,' and this is a simple technique. This is another form of DILD. Most people combine this technique with the MILD technique since this is one of the best ways to enhance lucid dreaming. The following are the steps to follow to perform this technique:

- Set the alarm for five hours after you have gone to bed.
- Take an hour before you go to bed to read more about lucid dreaming. This sends the right signals to your brain and stimulates it to remain active throughout your dream.
- When the alarm rings, do not open your eyes but force your body to go back to sleep while your mind is still active. Alternatively, you can also walk around while you focus on your dream.

There are a few more things you need to know about this technique.

As mentioned earlier, you have vivid dreams or lucid dreams during your REM sleep stage. Your first REM sleep state occurs an hour after you fall asleep, and you have additional REM sleep states every ninety minutes after the first state. The objective of this technique is to wake up during your REM state and go back to sleep as soon as you can. You should also ensure that you go back to your dream and stay aware that you are in a dream. It is best to visit a sleep lab or have someone watch you when you sleep. This is the best way for you to time your phases. You should repeat this method until you know when you are in your REM state.

Get Extra Sleep During Your REM State

You should sleep for longer during your REM sleep state. You can get some extra sleep during your REM sleep, and one of the most effective ways to do this is to stick to a sleep schedule. You must also ensure you sleep for as long as you can, so you wake up feeling refreshed and relaxed. It may be difficult to manage this, considering that, in the next step, you must wake up a few times each night. If you cannot go back to sleep immediately, you should look for a different method to use. Do not attempt this technique more than twice a week.

Wake Up

If you sleep for eight hours every night, you should set the alarm so it goes off four or five hours after you fall asleep. You are definitely going to be in a REM sleep state during those hours, but you cannot always pinpoint when it starts. The REM phases may last longer in later phases, and you may have more lucid and vivid dreams.

Stay Awake for Some Time

When you wake up, you should wake up and write your dream down in your journal, if you were having one. You can either walk around or get yourself something to eat. The objective is to ensure you remain conscious, and your mind is both alert and active. Your body, however, is still asleep and filled with the right hormones. Experts say that you can stay awake for as long as 30 minutes before you find it difficult to maintain lucidity in your dreams.

Focus Only on the Dream

You should focus on your dream before you go to sleep. After you have walked around for a bit, close your eyes and go to bed. If you could remember the dream you were having, you should recall that dream before you go back to bed. Visualize that you are back in the dream, and this may take some time for it to happen. There is, however, a decent chance that you may have this dream again.

Look for Other Ways to Concentrate

If you find it difficult to focus on your dream when you try to go back to sleep, you should use different ways to concentrate on your dream. If you do not remember anything about your dream, you can focus on some small movements, like moving your fingers. You should repeat this movement until you fall asleep.

MILD

MILD is an acronym for 'Mnemonic Induction of Lucid Dreams,' and it is best to combine this technique with WBTB. You need to concentrate when you use this method to practice lucid dreaming.

In this technique, you use mantras or phrases to help you convince your mind to maintain lucidity in your dreams. You can repeat this mantra, 'I know I am dreaming,' before you go to bed. This is the easiest way to convince your mind that you are only in a dream. You can also spend some time during the day to visualize a possible dream. You can tell your mind that you want to fly in your dream. Repeat this vision to yourself until you are sure the thought has manifested itself in your mind, or until you fall asleep.

This can take time to master, but if you are struggling, try to convince yourself that you must wake up immediately after your dream. Alternatively, you can use the WBTB method to do this. When you are awake, try to remember your dream, and make a note of it in your journal. Before you go back to bed, focus on your dream, and visualize it. You should use this technique only after you have practiced lucid dreaming for some time.

Autosuggestion

Autosuggestion is a highly effective technique and has been used in scientific research. This technique includes hypnosis, so only use it if you are comfortable with hypnosis. You use a mantra similar to the one we used in the previous chapter. You should repeat to yourself that you would have a lucid dream. Repeat this mantra continuously so that you convince your mind that you will have a lucid dream. Do not force this thought into your mind, since it can change the way your mind perceives the idea of lucid dreaming.

You can also use this technique to help you recall your dreams. Instead of telling yourself you will be lucid dreaming tonight, tell your mind that you will remember your dreams the following morning. When you focus on this thought, you can remember the dream the following morning. This method may be effective, but it does not work for everybody. If you want to improve the chances of success, use meditation to calm your mind down.

Follow the steps given below to use this technique:
- You should repeat to yourself every minute you get some time that you will have a lucid dream. This is the only way you can convince your mind to remain active during a dream.
- You can use any mantra. Consider the following:
    o I will know I am dreaming
    o I will have a lucid dream tonight
    o I will definitely be aware of everything in my dream

Continue to repeat this mantra until you go to bed. You must ensure you remain focused and make sure you say the same phrase repeatedly. This is the only way you can let your mind know you will remain active or lucid in your dream.

This may sound extremely simple, but this technique works best if you remember to be consistent. The only thing you must remember is that you should never force it. Do not force the lucid dream or the thought of a lucid dream, but let your mind become aware or lucid in your dream.

WILD

The WILD Method is the Body Asleep and Mind Awake technique that we talked about earlier in the book. This technique makes it easy for you to enter a state of lucid dreaming directly. Follow the steps given below if you want to use this technique:
- The first thing you must do is to lie down on your bed and close your eyes. Alternatively, you can wake up after four

hours of sleep. To do this, you should relax both mentally and physically.

      o The best way to relax is to meditate. This is one of the easiest ways to switch from your waking state to your dream state.

      o Make sure you do not move too much but relax.

- When you are relaxed and calm, focus on the darkness, and let your thoughts wander. You need to follow up on any thought or image that comes to your mind when you are in this state. This is known as hypnagogia. According to the Merriam Webster dictionary, "A hypnagogic hallucination is a vivid, dream-like sensation that an individual hears, sees, feels, or even smells. It occurs near the start of sleep." The only thing you must do is to relax and stay calm.

- Now, create your dream scene. When you let your thoughts carry you away, you can create the right scene for your characters and dream. Visualize your dream with as much detail as you can. Spend some time to look at the surroundings. This is the only way your awareness becomes higher.

- You are finally in the body asleep and mind awake state, where your body is asleep, but your mind is awake. When everything is finally in place, you will be dreaming. You move from a waking state to the dreaming state consciously.

Third Eye Method

The third eye method, also known as the Chakra method, is one of the common techniques beginners used to remain lucid or aware when they dream. If you use this technique, you must focus on your third eye chakra or the space between your eyebrows. You also need to follow a synchronized breathing pattern since it helps your mind relax. This makes it easier for you to become aware of your dreams. The third eye method is based on the WILD technique, and the only difference is this method uses meditation. Use this

method before you try the wake-induced lucid dream method. Follow the steps given below to practice this technique:
- The first thing you should do is go to bed and lie down. The objective of this method is to ensure you focus only on the energy in your third eye chakra. So, take deep breaths and focus on your third eye.
- Now, slowly begin to focus on having lucid dreams. When you fall asleep, your mind remains active and focuses on having lucid dreams. This is similar to the WILD step, and you can easily switch from the waking state to your dream state.
- The last thing you need to do is to focus on your breathing. You should focus on every aspect of your dream, so you have a lucid dream that night.

Chapter Eight: How to Explore your Dreamland

There are countless possibilities and scenarios you can explore in a lucid dream. Lucid dreams are not governed by the general principles of time and space regulating the physical world. However, some people are unaware of what they should do or where to start once they are in a lucid dream. If you don't know what to do after you get there, it defeats the purpose of lucid dreaming altogether. To make the most of your lucid dream, here are some simple suggestions you can use.

Start Flying

Channel your inner superhero and start flying! This is perhaps one of the exciting things you can ever try in a lucid dream. However, don't start flying unless you have stabilized yourself in the lucid dream. If you do it too quickly, chances are you will wake up. If you have ever wondered what it would feel like to fly like a bird in the sky, now is the time to explore it. To start flying, visualize that powerful energy is blasting off your feet, working against the gravity force, and pushing you upward.

Try Acrobatics

Do you want to swing from one vine to another like Tarzan? Or maybe leap from one building to another like the graceful cat woman? If yes, try acrobatics! You don't have to worry about physical injuries or fatally injuring yourself while you swing effortlessly like an acrobat. Jump from one high-rise building to another or even somersault to see how high you could go. Let your inner Cirque Du Soleil performer guide you.

Meet Celebs

Who wouldn't want to meet their favorite celebrities? Irrespective of whether it's a movie star or a football player, you can meet whoever you want in your dream world. All you need to do is merely visualize the person you wish to meet and believe they will be present somewhere in your dreamland. For instance, they could live on the street you have visualized, and you merely need to go to the specific house. After all, there are truly no limits when it comes to lucid dreaming, and there is no point in restricting or limiting yourself by the constraints of the regular world.

Try Teleportation

Anyone who has watched sci-fi movies is often intrigued by the idea of teleportation. Imagine how simple it would be to move from one place to another without lifting a finger. Instead, you will use the power of your mind. You don't have to travel physically, but all you need to do is think about a destination, and voila, you are there. If this idea fascinates you, there is no time like the present to start exploring it. Once you have induced yourself into a lucid dream, try teleportation. You can jump from one place to another, or even one world to another. It's quite easy; all you need to do is visualize the location you want to go to, and will it into existence. After you visualize the place, slowly start spinning, and believe you will reach the destination once you stop spinning.

Become A Movie Star

Why should you limit yourself to just meeting your favorite celebrities? You now have the power to become a movie star. If you want to be in a movie, you can create your own movie in the dreamland. You are the actor, director, producer, and scriptwriter. If there is a movie you love, you can try recreating it. If you want, you can also get other celebrities to star in this dream movie of yours. To truly experience the power of lucid dreaming, try to make your dreams as realistic as you possibly can. Visualize every little detail and experience all the feelings.

Dream Sex

If you have had sex before, it's quite easy to conjure all these feelings in your lucid dream. Lucid dream sex is quite thrilling, and it's one of the most incredible things you can experience. You should remember that if you are just getting started with lucid dreaming, save all the exciting things until later. Unless you learn to ground yourself in the lucid dream, any exciting activity you indulge in will merely wake you up. Therefore, first, concentrate on mastering the art of lucid dreaming before you dream about exciting things.

All in all, your mind is extremely powerful, and you need to keep in mind that you shouldn't keep visualizing the same person in all your lucid dreams. It can become difficult to distinguish between reality and memories of the dream world. You will learn more about things you shouldn't do in the dreamland in later chapters.

Thought Control

Wouldn't it be amazing and amusing if you could read minds? The ability to know what others are thinking is an exciting thought, and humans have been exploring this possibility for ages. You can look at someone and precisely know what they are thinking without any filters and feel what they are experiencing. If you want to do this, you can use thought control. Merely look at a fictional character in your lucid dream space and channel your consciousness from your body into the dream character to discern what they are feeling.

Shapeshifting

Why don't you try shapeshifting? You can transform yourself into any beast that walks the Earth. Maybe you can shapeshift into a cheetah and experience what it's like to be the fastest living being on Earth. Or perhaps you could transform yourself into the majestic blue whale. Maybe you could try transforming yourself into a fictional creature, such as the griffin or a dragon. Imagine what it would feel like to be a fire-breathing dragon soaring in the sky.

Move Away from Earth

Several scientific fiction movies have explored the idea of life on another planet. If any of these ideas have ever intrigued you, now is the time to test them. You have the power to move away from Earth and live on another planet. Why don't you try traveling to Mars or perhaps Jupiter? You have the freedom to fly wherever you want and visit any of the planets. If you want to get a little more creative, you can think about inventing your own planet!

Relive Memories

You probably have many fond memories that fill you with joy. With lucid dreaming, you get an opportunity to relive those memories. If there are any instances in your life where you wish you reacted differently or had a different response to the situation, try reliving them once more. When it comes to lucid dreaming, you have complete control over what you dream about and how the dream progresses.

Stand in Space

Do you want to feel like a cosmonaut out in the space? Well, now is your time to do this. If you want, you can also give yourself a bird's eye view of what the universe looks like. The world is certainly quite large, and it would look brilliant from space. Once you learn how to fly perfectly in your lucid dream, use this newfound superpower to travel upwards. Go through the stratosphere until you reach outer space.

Listening to Music

Anything you experience in the dream is more magnified than it actually is in reality. Therefore, even a small activity becomes more pronounced and profound. Something as simple as listening to music can be elevated and taken to the next level. If you want, you can organize a personal concert with your favorite singer or even listen to opera! In a vivid dream, if you listen to music, the overall effect is certainly amplified. All the emotions and small nuances of music we often miss in the real world are magnified in lucid dreams. Once you listen to music in your lucid dreams, it will truly change how you feel about it in the real world. Everything you experience in the dreamland will stay with you because you are conscious and aware of it all, even while dreaming.

Try Something New

Are you scared of stepping out of your comfort zone? If yes, trying something new in your lucid dream is a good idea. After all, a lucid dream helps create a safe environment to explore whatever you want without any worries. If you want to skydive, try doing it in a lucid dream. Even if you have never done it before, all the memories stuck in your mind from the videos you watched or the stories you heard can be replayed in the dream-like state.

Slow-Motion

We live in an incredibly hectic and busy world. Everyone seems to be in a rush and hurry to get somewhere or the other. As soon as you wake up in the morning, you need to get dressed and rush to work. Once work ends, you need to rush home. If you want to give yourself a break from all this rush, take a break and enter your dream world. You can live life in slow motion in lucid dreams. You have the power to slow down time and live life in slow motion. When you are extremely busy, it's highly unlikely you can notice the small things in life. For instance, you might not have the time to slow down and smell the roses. In a lucid dream, you have all the time you need to do all this. When you live life in slow motion, you can finally experience the beauty of sunrise and sunset, the chirping of birds, and the simple joys of nature.

Control Time

How wonderful would it be if you could control time? With lucid dreaming, you can revisit your past, explore the future, or connect with your present. Irrespective of what you want to do, you have the power to do it. You can slow time down and can control it, too. You can revisit a historical occurrence, rewrite history in your mind, or pay a quick visit to your future.

Opposite Sex

It is often said men are from Mars, and women are from Venus. Were you ever curious about what the opposite sex feels and thinks? Now is the time to understand what it would be like to live life as your opposite sex. You can do all this without expensive, painful, and complicated surgeries. Follow the same technique which was mentioned for teleportation. Visualize what you want to achieve, start spinning, and once you stop spinning, you would be transformed into your opposite sex. Do you remember the move, "Switch?" The lead character in the movie, an alpha male, is transformed into a woman. Well, you can try this too!

Explore Another Character

You can conjure up any character you want in your dream state and change into that character. In fact, you can transform yourself into any person you want to be. Why limit yourself to celebrities and famous people? You transform yourself into your best friend, partner, parent, or even an acquaintance at work. This is also a great way to understand how others think. You are literally placing yourself in someone else's shoes. If you have a tough time associating with others or are lacking in empathy, try this technique. You can safely explore your boundaries and those of others without any harm. Try to have conversations with this dream character or the person you are transformed into.

Another simple idea is to explore the mind of your dream characters. For instance, if you are out for drinks with your friends, imagine the scenario in your head. Try playing out what the other people would say while having a good time. This technique comes in handy while you are analyzing different relationships in your life. For instance, if you have doubts about whether a relationship is healthy or not, try doing this.

Survive An Apocalypse

Do you like watching movies about the apocalypse? Be it a zombie invasion, an alien attack, or maybe the end of the world, irrespective of what you like, you have a chance to experience all of it. Did you have fun watching a zombie movie? Imagine how much more fun it would be if you were actually a part of that movie? Another brilliant thing about this technique is you can use your other superpowers to defeat these zombies or monsters you have imagined. For instance, you can fly like Superman, channel your inner Hulk, or do anything else that you want to. However, while you do this, ensure the dream doesn't turn into a nightmare. Whenever things start getting scary, consciously regather your thoughts and change the script. After all, the purpose of a lucid dream is not to wake up in a cold sweat.

Find Your Spirit Guide

Perhaps one of the most interesting and brilliant things you can do while exploring a lucid dream is to find your spirit guide. Your spirit guide or guardian angel will keep you safe and help you find solutions to any problems you might be experiencing in life. At times, simply saying, "I want to find my spirit guide," does the trick. It is believed you need to ask the entity, "Are you my spirit guide?" thrice to confirm it is your spirit guide indeed and not a malevolent entity. You will learn more about this in the subsequent chapters. If the entity doesn't confirm it thrice, it is not your spirit guide. Don't forget this rule whenever you summon your spirit guide in the dream world.

Deal With Your Fears

Do you have any fears or phobias? Maybe you are scared of closed spaces or public speaking. Perhaps spiders or deep water scares you. Regardless of your fears, you can safely explore the cause of your fears in a lucid dream. Whenever you get overwhelmed or scared, you can end the dream or turn it into something pleasant.

Practice Real-Life Scenarios

Are there any real-life scenarios that intimidate or overwhelm you? Perhaps you were nervous about a big presentation at work, or a job interview. Or maybe you are scared about going on a date. Irrespective of what the circumstance is, you can rehearse and practice for it in your dream world. Instead of rehearsing all this in the real world, doing it in the dream world is easier. It also allows you to explore the same situation from someone else's perspective and not just your own. So, the next time you find yourself worrying about an interview, turn to your dreams, and things will get easier.

You can also train yourself to speak in front of large groups to get rid of any fear you have. A word of caution: don't try to experiment with too many real-life scenarios. You might reach a stage where you start believing you had done or said something in reality, when all you did was think about it in the dream world. You wouldn't want to be stuck in a situation where you believe you had an important phone call, only to realize it was just a dream.

Once you follow the different tips discussed in this section, you will truly enjoy lucid dreaming. However, be patient with yourself. Lucid dreaming is a skill you need to develop slowly. It can take a couple of attempts, but the results will leave you pleasantly surprised. Before you try any exciting activity, don't forget to ground the dream. After the dream has stabilized, allow your creativity to run wild and explore whatever you want.

Chapter Nine: Meeting Spirit Guides in Lucid Dreams

What Is a Spirit Guide?

Were there instances when you did something that made absolutely no sense, but it turned out to be exactly what you were supposed to do? Such instances often leave you wondering why you acted how you did. If you had such experiences in life, then it's an interaction with your spirit guide. A spirit guide is an entity that holds power and has the energy that it uses to communicate certain thoughts, feelings, responses, and healing to others. Spirit guides radiate positive energy and offer assistance in some form or another. They are known as guides because they assist in a situation by implanting a thought in your head to keep you safe. Spirit guides are also known as guardian angels. You can meet these spirit guides in your dreamland.

Types of Spirit Guides

Spirit guides could be in the form of ancestral guides, ascended masters, a common spirit guide, or even animal guides. An ancestral guide is an entity you have some form of relationship with or who is related to you and your family. It could be a long-dead ancestor or someone you were once close to and is no more. Anyone with your best intentions at heart and who has a kinship with you is often reincarnated as a spirit guide. Your ancestral guides are related to you by blood and are often believed to be guardian angels in different cultures.

An ascended master is an individual who performs reiki or any other energy healing. Ascended masters are physical beings who led a physical life but have moved on to higher planes of energy, such as Lord Krishna, Buddha, or even Jesus. Ascended masters often work with a group of souls and not just individual beings, unlike ancestral guides.

A typical spirit guide is often symbolic or representative of a specific guide and can take on the form of a storyteller, a wise crone, or even a warrior. They usually appear for a specific purpose. The purpose is often to teach you or prompt you to move on a good path. They can also help solve any problems you might be facing. Another common type of spirit guide you might encounter are animal spirit guides. Animal spirit guides function more like companions. For instance, you might meet a deceased pet who was there to help you through the grieving process. According to spiritual traditions prevalent in shamanic and certain Native American cultures, every individual has an animal totem or an animal spirit guide, which helps protect them from negative energies or acts as a guiding light.

Finding Your Spirit Guide

Now that you are aware of what a spirit guide is, try to concentrate on meeting one in your dreamland. There are different techniques you can use to meet one, but don't be disheartened if it doesn't work immediately. As with anything else in life, it takes some time, effort, and patience. Here are some simple tips you can use to find and meet your spirit guide.

Meditation

Meditation is a powerful tool because it helps connect your subconscious with the vast powers of the universe. Before you start meditating to find your spirit guide, ensure your mind is clear of all thoughts and clutter. Concentrate only on finding your spirit guide and nothing else. Don't think of meditation as a destination. Instead, it is a journey. To get started on this journey, visualize yourself in a serene forest, at the beach, a scenic mountainside, or anywhere that relaxes you. Don't think about anything else, and concentrate only on exploring the surroundings. While you start exploring the dreamscape, chances are you will bump into your spirit guide.

As mentioned in the previous section, your spirit guide is an archetype and could come in different forms. The spirit guide's form is merely a representation of certain characteristics and traits you value. For instance, your spirit guide could take on the form of Martin Luther King Jr. It doesn't mean he is your spirit guide but is a representation and embodiment of traits dear to you, such as freedom, resilience, and courage.

Look For Signs

A simple way to meet your spirit guide is to ask for a sign or an omen. Spirit guides sometimes make their presence known through symbols and signs. These symbols, signs, and omens can be quite basic or complicated. All you need to do is merely look for it. Unless you ask the spirit-guide a question, you will not get the answer you need. If you are stuck in a dilemma, ask for a suggestion or a solution, and once you have made your request, start looking for signs.

For instance, if you are considering shifting to a new place, but are scared about it, ask your spirit guide for some guidance. If you notice some signs such as a random conversation with a long-lost friend in the same city you are thinking about moving to, or maybe you notice vehicles with registration plates of the area you're thinking about shifting to, these are signs that can pop up at random times and places. All you need to do is consciously look for them. If you find these signs, it means a spirit guide is reaching out to you.

Dream Journey

A dream journey is quite similar to meditation and is also known as a vision quest. It is essentially a technique used to find your spirit guide via the subconscious mind. Unlike in meditation, where you are awake, the dream journey occurs in your dream state. You are asleep while going on this purposeful journey. Lucid dreaming can help you connect with your spirit guide. Before you sleep, concentrate on your purpose of finding the spirit guide, and focus on what you're trying to accomplish. If you meet someone during your lucid dreams, don't forget to note it as soon as you are awake. Write down your conversations, and all the information you obtain from the other person.

Intuition

Were there instances when a little voice in your head prompted you to do something? Maybe it told you it was time to move on, head in a different direction, or listen to what others said. The little voice that often talks to you is your intuition. Most of us are dismissive of our intuition, but it's quite powerful. The intuitive voice, which guides you in the right direction or prevents you from harm, could manifest as your spirit guide. To identify the presence of the spirit guide, listen to this inner voice, and evaluate the suggestions it gives you. If your intuitive ideas are right and helpful to you, it is your spirit guide trying to connect with you.

There are no hard and fast rules about spirit guides. You might have one or multiple spirit guides who take turns and appear in your life. Remember, a spirit guide appears only in times of need and not whenever you call on them. Unless there is a real need, a spirit guide might not show up, so don't get discouraged.

Connect With Your Spirit Guide

Guidance is always within your reach, but you will not receive it unless you expressly ask for it. If you need help to solve a problem or address a dilemma, ask your spirit guide for their help. The more you ask, the higher are the chances of receiving. It doesn't mean you shouldn't rely on yourself. It merely means you are asking for a little assistance to get where you want . A cab will not stop for you unless you flag it down by waving your arms; likewise, your spirit guides might not reach out to you because you haven't reached out to them. It is not just about asking; be sure that you listen to the advice given by your spirit guides. You cannot listen to them unless you quiet your mind and free up your mental clutter. Once you slow down, it becomes easier to connect with your spirit guide. You can use meditation to attain this objective.

You can ask your spirit guides for assistance by making a note of all the areas in which you need some help. Start with meditation and grab a journal. Write down your problem, ask the spirit guides for their assistance, and start writing down the thoughts that flow into your head. To seek your spirit guide's assistance, you can say something like, "Dear spirit guide of truth, love, and compassion, I welcome you to write through me, so I know what I am supposed to know."

Your job doesn't end here. After you seek guidance, you should also watch out for signs. As discussed in the previous section, spirit guides often offer guidance through different signs, symbols, and omens. Start looking out for these things.

Before you start blindly following the advice you receive from your spirit guides, it's important to test whether the entity you meet in the dreamland is your spirit guide or not. At times, malevolent energies or anyone else invading your dreams might show up as your spirit guide. So, pay close attention to the advice you receive. If you try the advice and nothing good comes of it, that's another sign you shouldn't ignore. Even if your spirit guide looks like your kin or someone you trust, being cautious is a good idea. If all the information you receive from the spirit goes against your beliefs, logic, or common sense, the entity you are interacting with might not be your spirit guide. You will learn more about protecting yourself from negative energies and dream invaders in the subsequent chapters.

Chapter Ten: 14 Things to NEVER Do When Lucid Dreaming

Lucid dreaming is fun and exciting. It allows you to do whatever you want and explore your creativity without any worries. Since you have the power to do whatever you want, it's important to stay in the right state of mind and have good intentions at heart. Even if it is safe, there are certain things you must never try during lucid dreaming. Just because you have the power to do anything you want, doesn't mean you should. The purpose of lucid dreaming is to explore your subconscious; learn, experiment, and explore. So, anything that isn't positive or constructive should be avoided. In this section, let's look at certain things you should never attempt during lucid dreaming.

Mistake #1: No Violence

Lucid dreaming is different from playing a violent video game. Remember, a lucid dream is not an episode of Grand Theft Auto. Every scenario you explore and the different people who feature in these scenarios are all extensions of your persona and subconscious. So, any violence against other entities in your dream is merely a form of self-harm. If you hurt anyone, you are merely hurting yourself, and this is undesirable. Since lucid dreaming is extremely vivid, any physical harm or violence directed towards others could stay fresh even after waking up.

Mistake #2: Lack of Planning

Planning is important in every aspect of your life, and a little bit of planning is important for dreaming, too. If you start lucid dreaming without a plan or a goal in mind, likely you'll merely end up standing there or forgetting what you're supposed to do. Therefore, before you start lucid dreaming, ensure that you have a specific goal in mind. It not only enhances your overall experience but also becomes a learning opportunity. Repeat your goal, right before you go to sleep, or think about it all day long. Once this goal gets embedded into your subconscious, it stays with you even in your dreamland.

Mistake #3: Extremely Exciting Activities

Indulging in extremely exciting activities can end the lucid dream. If your mind is too stimulated, waking up from the dream is quite likely. Before you try to do anything exciting, ensure you have stabilized yourself in the dream world and the dream itself. For instance, if you realize you're lucid dreaming, and your first activity is to jump into bed and have hot sex, it's unlikely the dream will continue. Chances are, you will find yourself wide-awake and restless in the bed. Before you try any of this, ensure that you have some practice over lucid dreaming. Once you've mastered the different techniques discussed in this book, indulging in exciting activities will become easier.

Mistake #4: Shutting Your Eyes

When you shut your eyes in the lucid dream, it awakens you. When you are lucid dreaming, you are viewing and experiencing things from your perspective. By shutting your eyes, you are ending that dream effectively. If your goal is to end the dream and wake up, then shut your eyes.

Mistake #5: Stop Thinking About Your Body

Focusing on the dream and staying in the dreamland when you are lucid dreaming becomes difficult if you keep thinking about your real-life body. If the only thought in your mind is about your physical body lying on the bed, how can you possibly concentrate on the dream? If you want to stay immersed in the dream and wish to reap the various benefits of lucid dreaming, stop thinking about your body.

Mistake #6: Avoid Real-Life Memories

Stop thinking about situations that are quite like your real-life memories or experiences. Here's a simple example: let's assume you are in a lucid dream, and you're talking to a prospective client. You have successfully negotiated the terms of a contract and have cracked the deal. If you are quite elated and happy when you wake up, you might believe the lucid dream was reality, and you cracked the deal. Why does this happen? Lucid dreams are quite vivid, and at times, these memories can get mixed up with your real-life memories. Therefore, the simplest thing you can do is to avoid thinking about memories which are quite similar to your waking life.

Mistake #7: No Bad or Negative Thoughts

Scary lucid dreams might sound intriguing and exciting. Do you want to avoid nightmares during lucid dreaming? If yes, avoid thinking bad or negative thoughts. Remember, a lucid dream is an extension of your subconscious. The simplest way to avoid any negative or bad thoughts from straying into your lucid dreams is to meditate or repeat positive affirmations before sleeping. A positive thought makes for a better lucid dreaming experience. Also, a lucid dream is not an escape or a coping mechanism. Deal with any problems you have in life before you try solving them in the dreamland.

A lot of people use lucid dreams to explore their darkest fears and worries. Or maybe you love the horror genre and want to see if you could survive your favorite horror movie. Initially, it would be best to avoid all negative and scary thoughts. You are in a special state of the subconscious during lucid dreaming. If you don't want to intensify your fears further, avoid thinking about them. You can attempt overcoming your fears once you get the hang of lucid dreaming. If not, you are merely inducing nightmares!

Mistake #8: Avoid Consistent Real-Life Individuals

People you know might feature in some of your lucid dreams. It is quite normal to dream about others you know. However, stop fixating or obsessing over a single person. If someone you know repeatedly appears in your lucid dreams, your mind will create fake memories. As mentioned in the earlier points, you can regulate your subconscious in the lucid dreamland. If you keep hanging out with a specific person in the dreamland, have several conversations, and do things together, your real-life memories become blurred. Your brain would be quite confused when you meet the said person in real life. You might also be disappointed when you don't feel the special connection you did in the dreamland. All this is due to confused memories. As a rule of thumb, avoid spending too much time in lucid dreams with people you know in real life.

Mistake #9: Stop Exerting Too Much Control

You can control and dictate the course a lucid dream takes. Having said that, exerting too much control would take away the magical experience lucid dreaming is supposed to be. If you are just getting started with it or don't have much experience, you cannot exert much control over your dreams. Do not get frustrated if you are unable to control your dream state. It merely means you need more practice to get the hang of it. It takes practice, consistent effort, and a lot of time. Once you're willing to commit to it and make the required effort, you will truly enjoy the benefits of lucid dreaming.

Mistake #10: Avoid Looking In Mirrors

What happens when you close your eyes or think about your real-life body? Both of these things will awaken you. Likewise, looking in a mirror does the same. It might be exciting, and you might be curious about seeing your reflection in a mirror during lucid dreaming. However, try to understand that mirrors don't function like they normally do in real life during lucid dreaming. If you are going to look in a mirror while dreaming, expect it to be different. At times, the reflection in the mirror might be a little scary, and it can wake you. Therefore, understand what you can expect and accept the fact the reflection might be a little scary. Once you are prepared, you will not accidentally wake up. Another likely scenario, you should consider is the mirror could reflect what you are feeling and your general state of mind. If you're in a happy state and thinking positive thoughts, the reflection would be more positive, and vice versa.

Mistake #11: Not Setting A Time Limit

Lucid dreaming is fun and exciting. However, be wary of the time you spend in the dreamland. If lucid dreaming is the only reason you go to bed at night or is the most exciting aspect of your day, something is wrong. As with anything else in life, there needs to be some balance. When unbalanced, things go haywire, and the purpose of lucid dreaming is defeated altogether. Don't use lucid dreaming as an escape mechanism. It is not a coping mechanism to deal with the realities of life. Instead, learn to deal with your worries and use lucid dreaming as a tool for exploring your subconscious. If you spend too much of your time and lucid dreams, you prevent yourself from living life like you're supposed to.

Mistake #12: Not Doing Anything

Not doing anything, merely exploring the dreamland or roaming around, is not a good idea. These activities help stabilize the dream, and that's it. Once you have stabilized the dream, start exploring the dreamland. If you do nothing, you are merely wasting an opportunity. Avoid any constant reality checks while in the dreamland. Enjoy the lucid dream because it is a magical experience. Doing nothing takes away the magic from this experience. It is one of the reasons why you must plan before you start lucid dreaming.

Mistake #13: Avoid Spinning Quickly

Before you attempt to do anything in the lucid dream, the first step is to stabilize the dream itself. A simple way to do this is to spin around in circles. While spinning, do it slowly and only for a while. If you do too much spinning, it might wake you up. To ensure you are dreaming, one or two reality checks will help. Don't go overboard, and don't keep constantly checking to see if you are in the dream state. Spinning too quickly can stimulate your nervous system and wake you up from the dream.

Another thing you should avoid doing is trying to fly when you are not yet ready. It might seem like a cool idea to fly in dreams. After all, we all thought about it at some point or another, and the lucid dreamscape gives you a chance to try it. If you're just getting started, avoid trying to fly. If you try doing it too quickly, your conscious brain kicks in, and you start asking yourself logical questions such as, "How can I fly?" or "I cannot fly because of gravity." These things will wake you up and can lead to a frustrating experience.

Mistake #14: Don't Think, "I Can Do It Later."

If you are aware you are in a lucid dream and feel like doing something, try to do it as soon as you possibly can. Chances are, you'll forget about it if you don't do it immediately. As soon as the lucid dream has solidified, work on enacting your lucid dream script. If you keep telling yourself you can do it later or feel like walking around for a while, you forget about it or, worse, wake up from the dream.

By avoiding these common mistakes, you can enhance your overall experience of lucid dreaming and reduce the likelihood of abruptly waking up from the dream.

Chapter Eleven: How to Protect Yourself While Lucid-Dreaming

It isn't necessary that every dream you have is a pleasant and happy one. You can have nightmares, too. There might be instances when you are lucid dreaming, and something doesn't feel right. Perhaps a disturbing entity or an image somehow entered your dream, and you didn't consciously give it the power to do so. What can you do in such situations? The good news is, there are some simple tips and steps you can follow to avoid any unpleasantness in your lucid dreamland. The two common sources of unpleasantness in lucid dreams are nightmares and dream invasions. In this chapter, we will explore these concepts and learn about tips you can use to protect yourself.

Nightmares

Were there dreams you woke up from with your heart beating rapidly and frantically? Dreams that leave you in a cold sweat? Perhaps you are being chased by a monster while you run to save your dear life. Or maybe you are living through your worst fears while feeling helpless and out of control. Both these instances can abruptly wake you up from your sleep, leaving you feeling anxious.

This brings us to the next point, the differentiation between nightmares and night terrors. Even if they sound similar, they are quite distinct. There are three primary differences between these two concepts. Night terrors often come during the early phases of sleep, while nightmares come at a later stage. Nightmares are often induced when your sleep is the longest, and your dreams slowly turn bizarre and are heavily influenced by the emotions you experience. Night terrors are associated with non-REM sleep, while nightmares are associated with REM sleep. When you have a nightmare, you will likely have a vivid recollection of the unpleasant dream. As far as night terrors are concerned, it's quite likely you'll only remember fragments of your experience or have complete amnesia about the episode.

Nightmares disrupt your REM sleep. It's believed the brain doesn't really stop thinking even while you are asleep. It keeps reviewing all the experiences you had, or memories from different networks that share similar experiences. It also updates certain neural networks and learns to cope with new behaviors even while you're sleeping. This is one of the reasons why you might have nightmares. Any turmoil you experience while you are awake may manifest itself as nightmares during your sleep. Learning to cope with your negative emotions during the waking hours helps reduce the chances of nightmares.

Also, remember, any form of emotional turmoil can cause nightmares, not just fear. There might have been instances when you experience anger, resentment, disgust, or even grief after waking up from a nightmare. Frightening dreams you experience could be the mental manifestation of harm due to perceived threats to your physical or mental safety. Even a threat to your self-esteem, confidence, or sense of security can trigger nightmares.

A simple way to relieve any negative emotion you experience during a nightmare is to rationalize. Lucid dreaming allows you to know you are asleep, and whatever you're thinking about isn't happening in reality. This gives you a simple sense of control. The next time you're stuck in a nightmare, and you're aware of it, think about the situation logically. For instance, if zombies are chasing you in your nightmare, remind yourself you are safe and in your own bed. Another simple technique is to close your eyes to awaken yourself from the bad dream. You have complete control over your brain and thought patterns.

As mentioned in the previous section, one of the common factors that trigger a nightmare is the stress you experience. Your brain actively tries to solve any problem you face, even while you are asleep. Your brain is essentially rehearsing itself to deal with the problem once you are awake. If you can calm yourself before you go to bed, the chances of nightmares reduce. Making simple activities such as yoga, meditation, exercise, a little "me time", or a relaxing bedtime routine can help reduce stress. Lack of sleep or any other form of sleep deprivation can stress your brain, which, in turn, triggers nightmares. Try to sleep and wake up at the same time daily.

To reduce physical and mental stress, stay away from alcohol, nicotine, and caffeine right before bedtime. These substances stimulate the mind. Excess stimulation right before bedtime can send your brain into a hyperactive mode. Another simple technique is to avoid watching any scary movies or reading about any frightening and disturbing events at night.

Another simple way to eliminate stress is by scheduling some worry time. Even if it sounds counter-productive, allocate about five-to-ten minutes of worry time daily. During this period, you can think about every thought that has been worrying you all day long. Instead of ignoring or repressing these negative thoughts, you can create an outlet to deal with them. Once you deal with any unpleasantness, the chances of nightmares will reduce.

When you are lucid dreaming, you have the power to change the script of any dream. If you are stuck in a bad dream, merely change it. To do this, you need first to realize you are in a state of lucid dreaming. For instance, a monster is chasing you in your dream, and you are running in a dark alley. Instead of concentrating on this, think of a happier place. Now, visualize that you are running toward the happier place. After all, you are the master of your dreamland.

Dream Invasion

Did you ever have dreams when you experienced someone else present in there? A foreign presence that wouldn't go away, and influenced the course of your dreams? Or maybe you were in someone else's dream? These things are known as dream invasions. A dream invasion can be an accidental invasion or a purposeful invasion. In a lucid dream, you are either wholly or partly in the astral plane. You are manifesting the dream on this plane, and it temporarily comes into existence. It's only temporary because once you open your eyes, and are fully awake, the dream ends. A dream also disappears if you decide to move away from the astral plane. In a dream invasion, another entity enters the space you've created and interacts with you. Others can invade your dreams via their lucid dreams, rituals, meditation, or even astral projection. Now, let's look at the types of dream invasions.

An accidental dream invasion, as the name suggests, doesn't involve any premeditation. At times, when you share a strong connection with someone, they might get the power to enter your dreamland. In fact, often, all the people involved in the dream are also dreaming. It's similar to a shared dream where someone else is placed in your dream without their consent. The invader has no intention to invade your dream and means no harm. It was merely an accident. Accidental invasions are quite common with empaths. An empath is an individual who can feel and experience what others are feeling and experiencing. If your empathy is high, it's quite likely others would be drawn into your dreams. It's an involuntary experience, and there is no harm in it.

A purposeful invasion is the opposite of an accidental invasion. Why would anyone intentionally invade someone else's dreamland? There are different reasons, and the most common one is to influence the other person's thinking. A dream occurs in the astral plane, and whatever you dream about often stays in your subconscious. Since your subconscious mind is responsible for all automatic responses, including physical and emotional ones, it's quite powerful. Your subconscious memory governs your primary instinct for survival, motivation, and any other emotional reaction. A purposeful invader is trying to control these things by triggering a specific response. A purposeful invader has the power to pull others into their dreams. This is pretty much what the movie Inception is based on.

Another common reason for dream invasion, especially purposeful invasion, is to absorb any emotional energy manifested during the dream state. Lust dreams and terror dreams are the two usual sources invaders use to attain this objective. The attacker absorbs any energy which is created by your body during these dreams.

A dream invasion might sound like a nightmare, but there's a subtle difference between these two things. In a nightmare, it's often your personal stress from real life that's manifested as a bad dream. Not just mental stress, but any physical stress you might be experiencing, such as an illness, pain, or any life-threatening situation could trigger nightmares. Nightmares are often abstract in nature and are usually self-contained. However, in a dream invasion, the nature of the interaction between you and the other being invading your dreams is quite detailed. A nightmare is often illogical because it's a mere manifestation of your fear. A dream invasion is seldom illogical, and you might even have persistent interactions with the other being.

Are you wondering what you could do if you are stuck in a dream invasion?

A dream invasion occurs when someone else has breached your personal energy field. To prevent this, learn to protect your energy field. It's similar to installing a security system on your house to keep yourself safe. A physical security system might prevent thieves and robbers, but a mental security system protects you from negative intentions, feelings, and psychic attacks from malicious entities. To strengthen and protect the energy field, here's a simple meditative exercise you can try.

Start by finding a comfortable spot for yourself. You can either sit down or lie on the floor. Close your eyes, keep your body relaxed, and start breathing slowly and deeply. Take a long, slow, deep breath through your nose and exhale through your mouth. Repeat this ten times or until you feel completely calm. Now, bring up your hands and cupped them together as if you are holding a tiny ball. Visualize that this ball you are holding is full of bright lights. The bright light it radiates is full of love and affection. Visualize this ball is slowly growing until it surrounds you. It's not just surrounding your body, but has spread into the entire space around you. You can see the edges of this ball shimmer like small bright diamonds. Now, hold onto this ball once again and look at how it beautifully glitters. Visualize that you are viewing yourself in this bright light. As you start concentrating on it, the flecks of glitter from the ball are leaving your hands, filling the space between the ball and your body. Take a deep breath and slowly open your eyes. This simple exercise is believed to bring about a sense of serenity and security. You can also perform this exercise in a lucid dream.

Start meditating before you go to sleep at night. Meditation helps enhance your overall energy levels and gives you a chance to access a higher energy plane. It essentially creates a safe environment where the attackers cannot follow you. If your dreams are constantly invaded, don't react or resist them; instead, simply assert your control in the dream world. Remember, your dreams are well within your control, and no one can do anything to you unless you give them the control to do so. Someone else has entered your space, and it is time to reclaim your space. Don't indulge in any conversations; merely disengage. Repeating a simple mantra such as, "You're not welcome here," or "I don't want you here," can effectively end dream invasion.

You also have the power to call on your spirit guide in the lucid dream. Your guardian angel is right around the corner, and all you need to do is merely call it.

Chapter Twelve: Five Advanced Lucid Dreaming Techniques

Lucid dreaming has several positive effects on the dreamer. From becoming more self-aware to developing confidence, the use of dreaming is a wonderful experience. In the previous chapters, you were introduced to a few techniques for inducing lucid dreams. After using these techniques, if you're thirsty for more or are curious to set out on a new adventure, you can use some advanced techniques for lucid dreaming. In this chapter, let's look at these techniques.

Technique #1: Astral Projection

As mentioned earlier, there is a relationship between astral projection and lucid dreaming. When you go on an astral journey, you are essentially projecting your consciousness into the astral world. You are traveling to different experiences and locations in real time without relying on your physical body. In a way, only your consciousness is exploring the different scenarios.

Those who perform astral projections often talk about it as an out of the body experience, almost as if they were ghosts. Astral projection is an intriguing concept, and you can experience it during lucid dreaming. Your dream world is based on your consciousness, while the astral world encompasses so much more than this. It isn't restricted to your personal space or time. It is the culmination of everyone's experiences in life. With astral projection, you can witness and experience events from the past, future, and present. Still, you aren't able to interact with anyone else's internal world. Here are the steps you should follow to explore the astral world during lucid dreaming.

- To get started with astral projection, you need first to enter the state of a lucid dream. To induce a lucid dream, use the WILD (Wake Induced Lucid Dream) method.
- Once the lucid dream starts, shift your consciousness back to the room where you are asleep. Look at your physical body while it's lying on the bed.
- Take a walk around the room and notice any objects you haven't noticed before. For instance, maybe you never paid any attention to a pen you keep in the room. After you have zeroed in on the object, shift all your attention to it. Carefully examine the object and observe every detail.
- After you wake up from the dream, re-examine the object. If the object is not there in the room, or if the details are different, it means you were not astral projecting, and it was merely an extension of your lucid dreams. If the object and all its details are the same, you have successfully astral projected.
- Now that you know how to perform an astral projection, the next time you are lucid dreaming, explore beyond your room. Walk around the house or even the neighborhood. Once you're awake, re-examine the details to ensure it was an astral projection. This is an advanced technique, and you might not get it right at once. Therefore, you need to practice to get better.
- The final test to determine whether you have successfully astral projected or not is to ask your friend to place an object in their house without telling you what the object is. Your

friend should tell you where the object is placed without giving more details. It needs to be in a place that's easily accessible, such as the nightstand, kitchen counter, or the dining table. If you have successfully astral projected yourself, you'll have entered their home and be able to describe the object in detail.

Once you have mastered this technique, you can project yourself to any place in the world. You're not restricted by the physical world's barriers and can traverse between time and space using your consciousness.

Technique #2: Meeting Your Parallel Self

According to the multiverse theory, there are several parallel universes in existence where your parallel selves reside. It is a complex theory, but a simplified version suggests infinite timelines are encompassing several parallel universes. It essentially means that there is a parallel universe where something else would've happened for anything that has happened in your life. It is quite similar to asking yourself how your life would have been had you not made a specific decision at a given point in time. For instance, how would your life have turned out if you did not move to another city? Would things have been different if you chose a different major in college? According to the multiverse theory, for every decision you ever made, there exists a parallel universe, and there are different versions of you living in different timelines.

As with astral projection, you can use lucid dreaming to explore different multiverses of your life. Here are the steps you should follow for this technique.

- Start by inducing lucid dreams by following any of the techniques discussed in the previous chapter.
- Once you are in the state of a lucid dream, concentrate on a specific event or a decision you made in life. Shift all your attention towards the specific experience and meditate on that experience during your lucid dream. Visualize yourself in a parallel reality.

- You can intentionally shift your consciousness to travel on a different path by transferring yourself to the moment and making a different decision. Another alternative is to transport your consciousness into the present moment intentionally but in another reality.
- After you revisit your personal timelines in multiple universes, start visiting alternate timelines of the history we know.
- Don't forget to note all your observations from your visits to the parallel universes after you wake up. It not only helps verify your experience but also makes it more vivid. This technique works brilliantly well because, in your lucid dreamland, there is infinite space and time available. This, coupled with all the unlimited parallel universes that exist, means that there's plenty of scope for exploration.

Technique #3: ALDIT

The Advanced Lucid Dream Induction Technique (ALDIT) is a hybrid technique designed to create an exciting lucid dreaming experience. Here are the steps you should follow.

- Before you start with this technique, try not to consume alcohol, or keep it to the minimum amount. Stay in a positive mood and don't engage in any emotional conflict. Avoid this technique if you are mentally preoccupied or stressed. Altogether, you need at least seven hours of sleep to practice this technique effectively. Before you awaken, you need four hours of sleep, and at least three hours afterward.
- After four hours, wake up and get up from the bed. You can set the alarm to go off if you are unsure whether you can wake up on your own or not.
- (Optional tip: if you want to enhance the overall experience, take 4-8 mg of Galantamine. It's ideal for all those who don't have a sufficient supply of acetylcholine, a neurotransmitter, in the body. This is especially true for all those who are over 50 years. If you are taking Galantamine,

ensure that you eat a light snack and drink some water or fruit juice afterward. If you have any pre-existing health conditions or a cardiovascular disorder, check with your physician before taking Galantamine.)
- Now, it is time to start meditating. You need to meditate for anywhere between twenty and thirty minutes to ensure your mind is free from clutter. Ideally, it would be best if you sat on a chair or sit down on the floor while keeping your back straight and your body relaxed.
- After you make yourself comfortable, it's time to relive a specific dream. Change your response according to what feels appropriate to you right now and see what the result is. Your new response might not show you an actual solution, but it can represent a developmental step towards attaining the final solution. For instance, in one of your lucid dreams, you were faced with an aggressor, but you didn't do anything. Now that you are revisiting this dream, you can assert your authority by standing up to the aggressor. Whatever the dream is, try to respond differently and let it unfold.
- After you have finished reliving the dream, it is time to wake up. You can set the alarm to help you do this. Don't forget to note the new dream after waking up (you can do this immediately or later). Now, it is time to go back to sleep.
- Before you shut your eyes and drift off to sleep, repeat an affirmation about what you desire to do. You can say something like, "I want to become more aware in my dreams and respond appropriately to all the scenarios I face."
- Start counting backward from 100. You might feel drowsy in this process and lose track of the numbers. It is okay if this happens; allow that drowsiness to take over.
- You might briefly lose consciousness along the way and might feel or hear a vibration. This vibration can appear and disappear; it is also a good sign. If you hear this vibration in your head, concentrate on this energy, and meditate over it. As

you start meditating, the energy will intensify. If this energy is present around you, you can also step out of your body for an out-of-body experience. This is known as a WILD (Wake-Induced lucid dream).

- If you don't hear this energy and merely fall asleep, it is known as DILD (Dream-induced lucid dream). If this happens, chances are you will be transferred to a state of lucid dreaming while asleep.

Don't forget to record your observations once you are awake. If you don't want to write it down, keep a digital recorder to record your experience while still fresh in your memory.

Technique #4: Dealing With Fears and Phobias

Fear is an extremely overpowering emotion that can overwhelm you in any situation. Fears are seldom rational, and therefore, giving in to your fear does you no good. Overcoming fears and phobias is not an easy process. The good news is that you can learn to overcome your fears using lucid dreaming. As mentioned repeatedly, in lucid dreams, you have complete control over the scenarios and their outcomes. No one else can regulate your dreams, and the power lies in your hands. If something seems unpleasant, you can put a positive spin on it. There are different techniques you can use to overcome phobias such as hypnotherapy. However, the simplest thing you can do is to tackle your fears in the dream world.

Here is a simple explanation that will give you a better understanding of how you can tackle your fears and phobias in the dreamland. Let's assume that you are scared of snakes. The slimy and slithery creatures trigger a primal fear unlike any other you have ever experienced. Since you have complete control over your dreams, imagine or visualize these scary snakes as cartoon characters. By reshaping how you view the source of your fear, controlling it becomes easier. By reimagining the snake as a cartoon character, you are essentially taking away its power over you.

Visualize that you are listening to the upbeat music from a cartoon series. Or maybe you can make the snake talk in funny voices.

The next time you start dreaming, summon a snake. The snake might look a little scary, or it might even be human-sized. Your heart might start racing, and a wave of overpowering anxiety get hold of your rational mind. Merely calm yourself, and remember you have complete control here. The snake will not attack you, and you can make it stop. For starters, why don't you reduce the size of the snake your imagination has conjured up? Next, try replacing it with the memory of a cartoon character. It might relieve a little of your fear and make you feel more empowered. The next step is to talk to this creature as if it were a rational human being. Maybe ask yourself what this snake represents.

Perhaps an accidental encounter in your past created this fear. Maybe it was a disturbing memory. By exploring the cause of this fear, tackling the phobia becomes easier. After a while, if you encounter the same creature in your subsequent dreams, consider exploring the reasons why it scares you. In a way, lucid dreaming is a source of simple therapy. Regardless of whether you are scared of heights, enclosed spaces, public speaking, or anything else, lucid dreaming helps create a realistic yet safe environment to deal with these fears.

Technique #5: Explore Your Personalities

We all have different facets to our personality. A simple challenge you can try to enhance your overall lucid dreaming experience is to conjure different facets of your personality. Why don't you interact with the joker or the philosopher who lies deep within your mind? A lucid dream and anything you experience in it is a mere extension of your subconscious. So, the characters you meet in the dreamland are also extensions of the psyche. Why don't you ask this dream character to tell you a joke that will make you laugh? Even in a two-way conversation with any dream character, you are essentially conversing with yourself. Therefore, if your dream character tells you a joke to make you laugh, you just discovered a side of your persona you probably were unaware of. If a lucid dream makes you laugh, you have come a long way and are getting the hang of lucid dreaming.

Now, it is time to seek out the philosopher within you. A great thing about lucid dreaming is that it helps create a safe environment where you can explore any topic, concept, or idea you want to, without any fears. After all, no harm can come to you when you are in complete control of all the situations and scenarios. If you have ever wondered about your purpose or what your life means, now is the time to explore all this. This might seem like a tricky challenge because you are essentially setting off on a quest to find answers to questions that might not have any answers. Or maybe they do, and now you have an opportunity to find the answers! Either way, it could be a brilliant learning experience. By getting philosophical in your dream world, the answers you obtain from yourself could be quite unexpected. These questions might be too heavy for real-life conversations, but you can safely explore them in your subconscious.

Conclusion

Lucid dreaming is a truly magical experience. It's a type of dream where you are fully aware of the fact that you are dreaming. It gives you an incredible opportunity to explore your dreamland and go on brilliant personal adventures and experiences. It also gives you a chance to reconnect your dreams and interpret them effectively. With lucid dreaming, you are the creator, writer, producer, and director of your own play.

In this book, you were taught the meaning of dreams and their meanings, about lucid dreaming and the different benefits it offers, and different lucid dreaming techniques. The techniques discussed in this book can be divided into two categories: beginners and advanced learning techniques. You were also given a basic introduction to the link between astral projection and shamanic journeying using lucid dreaming. This book also taught you simple tips to prepare yourself for a better lucid dreaming experience and explore your dreamscape. An intriguing concept discussed in this book is how you can meet your spirit guides in lucid dreams and what they could do for you. You were also given practical and simple tips about things you should never do while lucid dreaming and protecting yourself in lucid dreams. When all these topics are put together, it is the perfect book to explore lucid dreaming safely.

Once you get the hang of it, the benefits it offers are truly amazing. From enhancing your awareness to better self-control, preventing nightmares, and understanding your power to explore your creativity, you can do it all with lucid dreaming.

As with any other skill, it takes time, patience, and consistent effort. Once you are willing to commit yourself to this process, your efforts will pay off. This book will guide, mentor, and prepare you for a better lucid dreaming experience. With lucid dreaming, you can explore your creativity and delve into your subconscious. Remember, patience is key, and don't get frustrated, even if you stumble a couple of times. It is part and parcel of the learning experience.

Here's another book by Mari Silva that you might be interested in

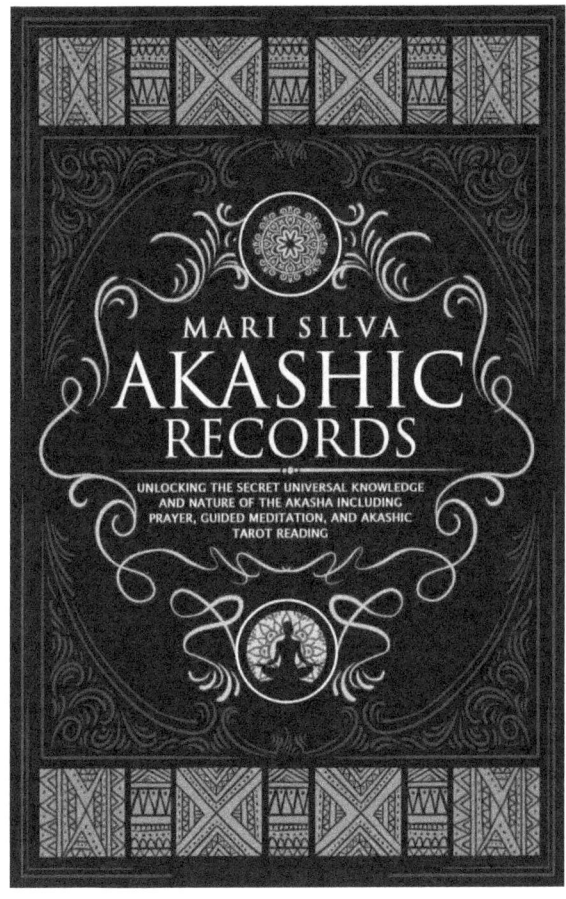

Resources

5 Great Benefits of Lucid Dreaming – USA TODAY Classifieds. (n.d.). Retrieved from USA Today website: https://classifieds.usatoday.com/blog/business/5-great-benefits-of-lucid-dreaming/

13 Things You Should NEVER Do In Lucid Dreams! (2019, June 8). Retrieved from www.youtube.com website: https://www.youtube.com/watch?v=bQK4jpeat-Q

40 Things To Do In A Lucid Dream, Especially Number 5. (2018, October 31). Retrieved from HowToLucid.com website: https://howtolucid.com/40-things-to-do-in-a-lucid-dream/

Antrobus, J. S., & Wamsley, E. J. (2009). Lucid Dreams - an overview | ScienceDirect Topics. Retrieved from www.sciencedirect.com website: https://www.sciencedirect.com/topics/neuroscience/lucid-dreams

Barrett, N. (n.d.). How to Lucid Dream. Retrieved from Gaia website: https://www.gaia.com/article/protect-yourself-from-psychic-attacks

Dimitriu, A. (2020, July 5). How to Lucid Dream. Retrieved from wikihow website: https://www.wikihow.com/Lucid-Dream

Ebben, M., Lequerica, A., & Spielman, A. (2002). Effects of pyridoxine on dreaming: a preliminary study. Perceptual and Motor Skills, 94(1), 135–140. https://doi.org/10.2466/pms.2002.94.1.135

Endredy, J. (2018, June 1). Shamanic Dreaming: How to Expand Into Higher Consciousness While You Sleep. Retrieved from Conscious Lifestyle Magazine website: https://www.consciouslifestylemag.com/shamanic-dreaming-lucid/

Hatfield, S. (n.d.). Dream Invasion. Retrieved from Samuel Hatfield website: https://samuelhatfield.com/articles/dream-invasion.html

Holecek, A. (n.d.). Five Benefits of Lucid Dreaming. Retrieved from Kripalu website: https://kripalu.org/resources/five-benefits-lucid-dreaming

Hoppler, W. (2017, September 19). How Guardian Angels Can Guide You in Lucid Dreams. Retrieved from Learn Religions website: https://www.learnreligions.com/guardian-angels-guide-your-lucid-dreams-123964

How to Have Lucid Dreams Easily - Learn Fast & Start Tonight. (2018, July 3). Retrieved from The Sleep Advisor website: https://www.sleepadvisor.org/how-to-lucid-dream/

How to Lucid Dream. (2017, April 18). Retrieved from Gaia website: https://www.gaia.com/article/protect-yourself-from-psychic-attacks

How To Lucid Dream In 2020 (WILD & DILD guides). (n.d.). Retrieved from Lucid Dream Society website: https://www.luciddreamsociety.com/lucid-dream-methods/

Hurd, R. (n.d.). Lucid Dreaming as Shamanic Technology | dream studies portal. Retrieved from https://dreamstudies.org/2010/09/14/lucid-dreaming-shamanism/

Léon D' Hervey De Saint-Denys. (2008). Les rêves et les Moyens de les Diriger : observations Pratiques. Paris: Buenos Book International, Dl.

Lucid Dreaming Frequently Asked Questions Answered by Lucidity Institute. (n.d.). Retrieved from www.lucidity.com website: http://www.lucidity.com/LucidDreamingFAQ2.html

Nunez, K. (2019, May 15). How to Lucid Dream: 5 Techniques, Benefits, and Cautions. Retrieved from Healthline website: https://www.healthline.com/health/healthy-sleep/how-to-lucid-dream#benefits

Nunez, K. (2019, June 17). Lucid Dreaming: Controlling the Storyline of Your Dreams. Retrieved from Healthline website: https://www.healthline.com/health/what-is-lucid-dreaming

Pavlina, E. (2006, November 13). Does Lucid Dreaming Lead to Astral Projection? Retrieved from ErinPavlina.com website: https://www.erinpavlina.com/blog/2006/11/does-lucid-dreaming-lead-to-astral-projection/

Renasherwood. (2011, November 21). Dreaming of Peter: Spirit Guides and Lucid Dreams. Retrieved from Dreaming of Peter website: http://dreamingofpeter.blogspot.com/2011/11/what-heck-are-spirit-guides-and-why.html

Review of Galantamine: The Lucid Dreaming Pill | dream studies portal. (n.d.). Retrieved from Dream Studies Portal website: https://dreamstudies.org/galantamine-review-lucid-dreaming-pill/

Sparrow, G., Hurd, R., Carlson, R., & Molina, A. (2018). Exploring the effects of Galantamine paired with meditation and dream reliving on recalled dreams: Toward an integrated protocol for lucid dream induction and nightmare resolution. Consciousness and Cognition, 63, 74–88. https://doi.org/10.1016/j.concog.2018.05.012

TOP 5 TECHNIQUES TO LUCID DREAM. (2018, June 27). Retrieved from Lucid Dream Society website: https://www.luciddreamsociety.com/top-ways-to-go-lucid-dream-now/

Turner, R. (n.d.). 52 Ways How to Lucid Dream - Mindset, Methods & More. Retrieved from www.world-of-lucid-dreaming.com website: https://www.world-of-lucid-dreaming.com/how-to-have-your-first-lucid-dream.html

Turner, R. (n.d.). Advanced Lucid Dreaming. Retrieved from www.world-of-lucid-dreaming.com website: https://www.world-of-lucid-dreaming.com/advanced-lucid-dreaming.html

Turner, R. (n.d.). Dream Induced Lucid Dreams (The DILD Method). Retrieved from www.world-of-lucid-dreaming.com website: https://www.world-of-lucid-dreaming.com/dream-induced-lucid-dreams.html

Turner, R. (n.d.). Lucid Dreaming Techniques for Beginners. Retrieved from www.world-of-lucid-dreaming.com website: https://www.world-of-lucid-dreaming.com/lucid-dreaming-techniques.html

Turner, R. (n.d.). The Official Lucid Dreaming FAQ. Retrieved from www.world-of-lucid-dreaming.com website: https://www.world-of-lucid-dreaming.com/lucid-dreaming-faq.html

Turner, R. (n.d.). The Cycle Adjustment Technique: Lucid Dreams with CAT. Retrieved from www.world-of-lucid-dreaming.com website: https://www.world-of-lucid-dreaming.com/cycle-adjustment-technique.html

Warnings from Sleep: Nightmares and Protecting The Self. (2017, April 13). Retrieved from Farnam Street website: https://fs.blog/2017/04/nightmares-and-protecting-the-self/

Wigington, P. (2019, April 28). 5 Tips for Finding Your Spirit Guide. Retrieved from Learn Religions website: https://www.learnreligions.com/find-your-spirit-guide-2561603

Wilson, M. (n.d.). The Picower Institute for Learning and Memories. Retrieved from picower.mit.edu website: https://picower.mit.edu/matthew-wilson

What Not to Do in a Lucid Dream - 15 Things (2020) - Lucid Dream Society. (n.d.). Retrieved February 24, 2020, from https://www.luciddreamsociety.com/ website: https://www.luciddreamsociety.com/worst-lucid-dream-ideas/

What is the Difference Between Lucid Dreaming and Astral Projection. (n.d.). Retrieved from www.ennora.com website:

https://www.ennora.com/blog/difference-lucid-dreaming-astral-projection/

www.ingramcontent.com/pod-product-compliance
Lightning Source LLC
Chambersburg PA
CBHW070046230426
43661CB00005B/780